PEL

THE GROWTH
IN SCO

Keith Webb was born in Kent in 1943 and is married with two children. He graduated from the University of Keele in 1970 and went on to post-graduate study at the University of Strathclyde. This was followed by two years at the University of Iceland lecturing in politics and a further year at Strathclyde. At present he is a Research Fellow in the Department of Systems Science at the City University, London. His other interests include the study of conflict and the problems of industrial democracy.

KEITH WEBB

The Growth of Nationalism in Scotland

WITH A FOREWORD BY
NIGEL TRANTER

PENGUIN BOOKS
IN ASSOCIATION WITH MOLENDINAR PRESS

Penguin Books Ltd, Harmondsworth, Middlesex, England
Penguin Books, 625 Madison Avenue, New York, New York 10022, U.S.A.
Penguin Books Australia Ltd, Ringwood, Victoria, Australia
Penguin Books Canada Ltd, 2801 John Street, Markham, Ontario, Canada L3R 1B4
Penguin Books (N.Z.) Ltd, 182–190 Wairau Road, Auckland 10, New Zealand

—

First published by Molendinar Press 1977
Revised edition published in Pelican Books 1978

—

Copyright © Keith Webb, 1977, 1978
All rights reserved

—

Made and printed in Great Britain by
Cox & Wyman Ltd
London, Reading and Fakenham
Set in Intertype Times

To Wanda

Contents

Foreword

This is a valuable and important book, especially in present circumstances. It could scarcely be more topical or more necessary. At the time of writing this, Scotland is poised on the brink of major developments. Whatever the fate of the devolution issue, as it is called – a depressingly dull and bureaucratic phrase for something strong and vital which should instead ring out like a trumpet-call – the clock cannot now be turned back. Scotland is on the march and will manage her own affairs again, in whatever degree; there are few things more sure than that. The politicians may botch and fumble it, but like Canute 900 years ago – who also thought the Scots were better governed from the South – they cannot turn back the tide.

It has long been my strongly held view that the Scots, in these circumstances especially, ought to know their history a great deal better. And that goes for their recent as well as long past history, and the story of the struggle for national identity and self-government which has brought us to where we stand today – or better, from where we stride forward. That is what this book sets out to do, and does it coolly, factually, impatiently, as is required, compared with the more emotive contributions of others. Not as *I* could have done it, admittedly, who am something of a partisan, an enthusiast, a flag-wagger if you like, by nature. This is a closely researched and careful study, taking care not to get bogged down in personalities – always a prime danger in any work dealing with the Scots and their affairs – and certainly the risk was there, with so many highly colourful and dramatic characters active on this particular stage. If the author credits one more than another in their devoted efforts to bring us to where we are now, he manages to hide his preferences – perhaps almost too well.

In the recent so-called 'great debate on devolution' one aspect
of it all has been made abundantly clear, however much else is
lost in verbiage, and that is the sublime ignorance of our legislators as to the entire subject, as well as their serene lack of
interest until the very last moment. Taken eventually by surprise,
and appalled, the Westminster Parliament suddenly discovered
a yawning abyss developing north of the Tweed and Esk, and
rushed to man the ramparts with almost hysterical fervour – this
despite the fact that the self-government movement in Scotland,
long so moderate, reasonable, constitutionally correct, has been
pleading itself hoarse with appeals, petitions, representations,
covenants and memoranda, directed at the selfsame politicians
all this century. I myself was one of the Commissioners nomi-
nated by the Scottish National Assembly in 1948 to inform the
Westminster parliamentarians of the desires and recommend-
ations of the Scots people, two million of whom were to sign the
Scottish Covenant.

We cannot divorce the long backlog of our history from the
present situation, even if we would – and we are alleged to be a
historically-conscious people, too much so for some of our
critics. The struggle of a comparatively small nation to maintain and cherish its distinctive identity, when sharing an island
with a people almost ten times as large, has been going on for a
thousand years. The more I delve into the past, the more clear
becomes the continuity and the similarity of the struggle. Only
the means and the methods change, on both sides. There is
something strong in the Scots national character which insists
always on surviving and the means of survival. I do not suggest
for a moment that as a people we are better or more worthy
than our neighbours – only that we are *different*, and have down
the ages always sought to ensure that that difference continued.

The birth of our national consciousness can probably be
traced back to the ninth century, when the Picts and Scots
united – possibly earlier, for our knowledge of our Pictish ancestors and their Alba is shamefully scanty. But out of that
union a new nation was born, the Kingdom of Scotland. And
almost immediately the attacks on it commenced, from the

Northumbrians, the Danes, the Vikings. But the first really major threat, of more than sporadic warfare, the threat of over-weening southern influence, did not occur until the mid-eleventh century. Then, on the death of King MacBeth, the last truly Celtic monarch of a Celtic polity, his successor Malcolm Canmore, a Celt himself but reared in England and presently married to an English princess, the famed Margaret, delib-erately sought to put down the Celtic polity and culture and to substitute the Romish for the indigenous Celtic Church – and succeeded all too well. A policy eagerly carried on by his sons who succeeded to the throne one after another – known significantly as the Margaretsons, where their father had been known as Malcolm Canmore mac Duncan. Some will declare that this beginning of Anglicization was good for the Scots; that has always been averred, down the ages. But that is not the point.

For this was the period of the Norman Conquest of England, and those vigorous invaders did not fail to turn their eyes north to Scotland. David the First, the youngest of the Margaretsons and the longest-reigning, welcomed them with open arms, and the Normanization of Scotland began in earnest. It was, of course, confined to the nobility and landed classes; but since they ruled the land, or the Lowlands at least, the effect was enormous. It is nevertheless one of the most extraordinary and at the same time hopeful features of our history, how even the Normans in their turn were conquered, absorbed, and trans-formed into Scots themselves. It took time, to be sure, as Wall-ace and Bruce found to their cost, in the Wars of Independence, when the English changed their methods to full-scale armed invasion and occupation. But gradually the Norman families were hammered, as were the rest of our people, into true Scot-tishness – as such Norman surnames as Lindsay, Fraser, Gordon, Comyn or Cumming, Seton, Sinclair, Montgomerie, Ramsay, even Stewart and Bruce itself, bear eloquent witness.

But the threat remained; and we do not have to look merely at the long tally of battles, from Homildon Hill in 1402 to Flodden in 1513. For open warfare was never so dangerous as was the

more subtle pressure and tendency, continual, unrelenting,
from the capture and English indoctrination of young James
the First, the royal marriages, the Rough Wooing of Henry the
Eighth, the Reformation influences from the already Reformed
South, the effects of the Union of the Crowns and the sovereign's
removal to London, the religious hegemony which produced
the Covenants, National and Solemn League, the blunt Crom-
wellian domination and indoctrination, the dichotomy induced
by the Jacobite loyalties and the Protestant Succession, right
down to the final – but not fatal, never fatal – loss of Scotland's
ancient parliament in 1707. Indeed the entire panorama of our
troubled history. In all of it the national identity was threatened
and threatened again; yet it always survived. Much was lost,
admittedly – but not the essential idea of nationhood, the urge
to control our own destiny, and above all the idea of freedom.

Little of that long struggle appears in this book; that is not its
purpose. But it can always be sensed, inferred, in the background. And if politicians cannot understand it, and seek to
equate the Scottish needs and aspirations with those, say, of the
North of England, East Anglia or even Yorkshire and other
English regions, then they but reveal their own ignorance and
complete lack of perception.

Yet this work is not basically for the politicians, however
much they may need it, but for the ordinary folk of Scotland,
all who have any interest at all in the state and future of their
land. And, with the Scots, as has been indicated, that means us
all. Also, to be sure, it is for our good friends and neighbours
south of the Border, most of whom probably are only a little
less bewildered than are their paid representatives.

I commend it to all.

Nigel Tranter
Aberlady 1977

Acknowledgements

The author would like to thank the following for their help and suggestions:

James Kellas of Glasgow University, Professor Richard Rose, Jack Brand, William Miller, all of the University of Strathclyde, and Eric Hall and Chris Harvie for the recent illuminatory work they have done on Scottish nationalism and upon which I have drawn heavily. There are many others too numerous to mention in the space available.

The many members of the SNP who gave their time over a number of years, in particular the late Oliver Brown, Mr and Mrs Spence, Dr and Mrs John MacDonald, Muriel Gibson and many others.

Hamish Whyte for bibliographical assistance and indexing, and Simon Berry of The Molendinar Press for the constant imposition of deadlines by means of which this book came to be published in 1977.

Finally, all fellow research workers (in particular Christopher Mitchell) on the Community Conflict Project at the City University for their forbearance whilst one of their number pursued a private hobby horse.

CHAPTER ONE

Introduction

For many years Britain was perceived by the world as a near-perfect example of a state based upon the class system. The major divisions in society were seen as being between social classes rather than between regions, cultures or religions. In spite of the Irish troubles following the First World War, and periodic rumblings from the Welsh and Scottish peripheries, the myth of cultural and ethnic homogeneity continued to be propounded. In Ulster today violence is a regular occurrence, caused by religious differences and Irish nationalism. In Wales the militancy of the Welsh-speaking minority has grown, as has their effectiveness. But, most importantly, in Scotland there has developed a mass political party with sufficient support to threaten the very unity of the United Kingdom.

Scottish nationalism is important in a number of respects. It will undoubtedly lead to great constitutional changes, the extent of which may not be apparent in the immediate future. Even though Parliament may reserve to itself the right of final decision, a Scottish Assembly could – by posing a constant threat to the unity of the British state – erode the principle of parliamentary sovereignty. The realities of power may enable the Scots, invoking the principles of their own legal system, to claim that their national rights are based upon fundamental law. It is likely that the Scottish question will also confirm the referendum as an acceptable constitutional device to resolve political problems which threaten to divide parties. Further, the introduction of proportional representation in Scotland, in order to protect the 'English' parties, could well increase the demand in England with far-reaching effects on the nature of British government. And, of course, by creating a Scottish Assembly with wide powers and conceding the right of Scotland to some measure of self-determination, the Westminster Government may unwittingly be fuelling the next stage of a developing nationalism.

Economically, the existence of such a strong political movement in Scotland strikes at the heart of British hopes of industrial and economic regeneration. The discovery of oil in the North Sea has had psychological effects at least as important as the predicted economic benefits: Westminster would not readily cede control of the oilfields to an independence-seeking Scottish Assembly. Conflict between the two legislatures is inevitable, given the present strength of nationalism in Scotland; it is therefore plausible to foresee debate about the amount of Central Government expenditure in Scotland escalate into argument about the distribution and ultimate control of the enormous oil revenues.

Ideologically, the trend to centralism – an increasing bureaucratic control emanating from Westminster – could receive a strong challenge. The recent local government reorganization, which created mammoth new councils, has also provided a focus for regional discontent in England. If Central Government perseveres with its attempt to buy off the nationalists by means of disproportionate expenditure in Scotland, the English regions may come to believe that their only protection lies in regional legislative devolution in England. In a European context Scottish nationalism may also present something of a problem. Given the small population and large energy resources of Scotland (the nationalists will be able to promise considerable comfort to security-conscious, oil-hungry nations in return for a measure of recognition. Further, their very presence and success may stimulate and encourage movements for regional autonomy elsewhere. Bretons, Corsicans, and even the Basques could learn the advantages of efficient organization and grassroots mobilization. Scottish nationalism is manifestly important but as yet we can only hypothesize about the consequences flowing from its success.

Nationalism as a theoretical concept is difficult to come to grips with. It is amorphous, ubiquitous and multi-dimensional.

It has been described as the most powerful influence in the post-Reformation world. It has shaped the modern world and defined the mode of interaction between its peoples. In spite of the long history of nationalism and its continuing activity in the contemporary world, with the considerable attention devoted to it by scholars, there is still debate about what it is and what causes its emergence as a political force. Its extreme variability is the problem: it can be found in any number of forms in very different circumstances. The cultural attributes upon which it may be based can vary greatly or be wholly absent. The ideologies it encompasses can be drawn from any point of the political spectrum. The relationship between the emergence of nationalism and any particular stage of economic development or social modernization is not constant. In the light of such variability the construction of any general theory of nationalism is a very difficult task.

In one sense, of course, nationalism needs no explanation. Basic to all nationalisms is a sentiment, sometimes called patriotism, sometimes chauvinism. This sentiment recognizes an entity, the nation (this may or may not also be a state) to which strong loyalty is owed. Often this feeling is sufficiently powerful that the individual may sacrifice his life in defence of the nation. Such sentiment is nothing new, however, for it existed long before the idea of a nation was clear. In the past, loyalty just as intense was given to the tribe, the village, a particular family or even to a region or religious group. The sentiment that divides the world into Us and Them on the basis of group membership is probably as old as human association and needs no explanation. The problem that has particularly exercised scholars is how this sentiment became focused on an entity as abstract as the nation. This is probably more difficult to explain historically than with contemporary nationalisms. Currently our thinking is so constrained by our political environment that it is difficult to think of a world not divided into nations. The nation has become a basic unit in our political thought, and where there is discontent on a wide scale it is not surprising that it expresses itself in these terms.

The history of nationalism is filled with conquest, subjugation and bloodshed. Sometimes such activities are justified in terms of personal or national freedom, or sometimes in terms of integration. While nationalism has been so important over the past three centuries and has often led to great suffering, there are now those who see the age of nationalism coming to an end. This is not a new hope. Much of nineteenth-century sociology made similar predictions, based either on the growth of class consciousness, which would come to supersede national loyalties, or upon the spread of industrialization, which would make diverse peoples increasingly similar culturally and in their social and political organization. There is little evidence to support either of these projections. When the crisis comes, loyalty to nation has always proved more powerful than loyalty to class: there would seem to be more that unites us than divides us. The spread of industrialization has not led to any great degree of similarity, but has on occasion – through the competition for markets and resources – led to some of the most militant and violent expressions of nationalism.

Contemporary optimists base their hopes on the growth of international cooperation and the spread of a world culture. Cross-national organizations such as the EEC are cited as evidence of this, and it is suggested that in time nations will become as regions in the new supra-national political organization. However, the growth of supra-national institutions may well have the effect of stimulating dissent among cultural minorities whose influence and ability to maintain their difference contracts in relation to the larger community. The growth of an international culture is proposed on the basis that the various forms of mass media are becoming increasingly cross-national in their operation. The effect of this is to spread and promote a similar view of life, to raise similar aspirations and hopes, and to suggest similar standards of prosperity and material satisfaction. By shrinking the world through speedy and efficient communications, different cultures are brought into contact and the differences rendered acceptable. But such a view ignores a number of factors. Close contact between different peoples has not always resulted in harmony; just as often it has resulted in slavery, exploitation and hatred. In addition, however similar attitudes may be, there will remain substantial national conflicts of interest. Prosperity at present is attainable by only a minority of the world's population and is maintained by a disproportionate share of resources. Further, cultural differences can be a source of great pride and many nations are actively fighting against what they see as assimilation and cultural contagion: this world culture is often seen as being a culture of Western Europe and the Anglo-Saxon nations. Also, many governments see the growth of international communications as a threat to internal stability and through censorship try to isolate their people from this contamination. There is therefore little reason to suppose that nationalism has run its course. It is probably as powerful today as ever.

Nationalism is sometimes considered as an ideology in its own right, although it differs in important respects from those bodies of thought that we normally consider as such. In common with other ideologies, it usually incorporates a view of history which is more or less mythical and idealized. It will also stress the peculiar qualities or genius of a people by virtue of which the right to self-determination is demanded. The nation is always seen as unique, and its special qualities can only be expressed in the context of political autonomy. It will also lay down the criteria of membership, especially in terms of the commitment required of the individual. Nationalism will also imply a claim to resources and define the material interests of the people. Since the land mass of the world is largely divided into competing nations, nationalism is going to be a potential source of conflict wherever there are scarce resources. What differentiates nationalism from other political ideologies, however, is that it implies nothing specific about the internal organization of the state or nation. Neither does it have anything to say about the mode of economic distribution. Nationalism has an almost infinite capacity for coexistence with other political doctrines, even those which are theoretically very much opposed to nationalism. In this sense nationalism is ethically neutral: it is found in both totalitarian and democratic states and is indifferent to the political complexion of the regime. The doctrines that associate with an emerging nationalism are to be explained more by the context and nature of the struggle, and the history and culture of the society, than by any guiding concept of nationalism.

The attributes upon which nationalism is based, or the social cleavages that it mobilizes, are also variable. Nationalism claims that a particular group is in some way unique and has interests that are only served through autonomous political expression. This quality is sufficiently general and important to subsume other cleavages of lesser importance, such as class, caste or religion. In nineteenth-century Europe this uniqueness was thought to reside in language. Those who spoke the same language saw the world in similar ways and thus formed a 'natural' or organic unity. In time, however, it became clear that nationalism could divide linguistic groups and could incorporate many dialects and languages. The term *language* became used metaphorically: 'to speak the same language' has much wider implications than mere verbal usage. It can imply similarity along some important dimension of life that aids communication and allows interaction to occur between otherwise dissimilar groups. The attributes that are held to distinguish a people will vary greatly between cases. A national unity can be postulated on the basis of a common history, a shared colonial experience, religion, language, culture, region, or even colour.

Since we are often dealing with large and diverse populations, the criteria for setting the boundaries of a nationalism are often blurred at the edges. This is not important, for nationalism like other ideologies is capable of redefining reality to accord with the aims of the movement. As one eminent sociologist commented in the 1930s, 'what people believe is real, is real in its consequences'. It is not the case that a verifiable unity need exist for nationalism to arise within a population. Nationalism can, upon occasion, create the sense of unity upon which it feeds. Sometimes, by presenting a different but plausible interpretation of the world, by reorientating popular perspectives, nationalism can channel existing discontent to its own ends. The qualities by which a people may claim to be a nation may well exist, but this perception of uniqueness may also be created by nationalism. Once the transfer of allegiance to the nation is accomplished, the mythical nature of that attribute becomes irrelevant.

Given the number of actual or assumed attributes upon which nationalism may be based, it is clear that there exist many potential nationalisms. What is it that causes only some of these possibilities to become actualities? The answer is again difficult: large-scale social events are invariably multi-causal, often the outcome of a myriad of smaller and unnoticed incremental changes. In addition, an event which appears to have particular causes in one situation appears to have wholly different causes in other circumstances. The position is complicated with regard to nationalism in that the process of nation-building has been going on for many years, and the earlier examples are in many ways very dissimilar from the newer, emerging nationalisms.

It is normally possible to point to some fairly common factors. For example, there is usually an economic dimension to nationalism. Although this can vary a great deal between cases, economic matters usually have a prominent place in pre-independence nationalist rhetoric. Nationalism may be the response of a relatively advanced section of a society, or it may be the expression of a region that sees itself as deprived and exploited. In either case there is usually perceived a disjuncture between the exercise of political control and the material interests of the region or people. Again, for nationalism to emerge it is necessary for there to be a group of people to spread the nationalist gospel. Often, although not always, such people are socially displaced, perhaps an educational elite for whom there is no place in the administrative structure of society congruent with their self-perceived capacities, or a commercial class excluded from power in a rigidly stratified, traditional society. In other cases it may be the military who feel they are not accorded the status and prestige that is rightfully theirs. Further, for nationalism to gain a mass following there must be discontent that can be focused into action or causes for discontent that can be highlighted.

One of the advantages that nationalism has over other militant social doctrines is that it has the power to unify many forms of dissidence and present them as having a single cause, while other ideologies tend to divide and polarize society. Whatever else may trouble and factionalize a people, they can be as one in nationalism. Like all doctrines of social change, an emerging nationalism attempts to alter perspectives of those it appeals to; it offers them alternatives which were not earlier perceived and thus gives them a standard by which to compare the present. Sometimes nationalism is the result of widespread changes in society, especially changes due to industrialization and modernization. The displaced worker or peasant in an industrial setting is confused by the loss of his traditional expectations. Nationalism can fill the void.

Nationalism, further, needs organization to be successful, as do all social movements. The form of the organization will vary according to the circumstances, particularly with regard to the degree of repression the Movement experiences. Repression may also set in motion the 'malign spiral' whereby the suppressive activities of the regime in response to dissident behaviour are seen to confirm accusations made by the dissidents, and thus strengthen the Movement. Nationalism will also tend to emerge where there is some expectation of success. This might be due to the weakness of a distant colonial power or possibly just a failure of will. Or it might be due to the fact that similar movements elsewhere have been successful, or through the use of some external military or moral support.

It is not the purpose of this book to investigate the general nature of nationalism, nor to place Scottish nationalism within the context of any particular theory. Rather this is a brief description of some salient aspects of the development of nationalism in Scotland. However, it might be noted in passing that in the generalized context of nationalism the Scottish case presents some unusual features. The level of hostility, for example, is very low. Englishmen and Scotsmen live and work together with little or no discord. In addition, it seems possible to suggest that, even though there is a powerful nationalist political party in Scotland, the level of discontent with the existing form of government is not high. In opinion surveys a large majority of Scots regularly choose many other issues facing government as being more important than the devolution question. Neither would it seem possible to argue that the degree of economic change has been sufficiently disruptive to fuel a nationalist movement. The discovery of oil in the North Sea certainly does not qualify in this respect, for nationalism was on the move long before. Nor can it be plausibly suggested that the leadership of the SNP is in any way a displaced intelligentsia seeking a place in the sun. The contemporary leadership is firmly embedded in the structure of Britain.

While the development of nationalism in Scotland does present some problems, it is not inexplicable if changes in the nature of government and the British party system are seen from a Scottish perspective. A primary point to note is that the sudden and recent upsurge of political nationalism in Scotland does not mean that a strong sense of Scottishness has only recently emerged. Rather, the Scottish sense of national identity has now become relevant to politics. In the past the Scottish identity and the British identity coexisted; they rarely conflicted because each was seen as being applicable to different areas of life, and politics was seen in a British context. The maintenance of the Scottish sense of identity through so many years of union with England can be attributed to a number of factors, not least of which is that some of the central institutions of the Scottish state persisted after the Union. Further, since the middle of the nineteenth century there has been considerable institutional growth and administrative devolution to Scotland, even though there also existed strong centralizing tendencies. This has meant that within the political framework of the United Kingdom a specifically Scottish interest has been delineated, partly because such developments have acted to stimulate and focus Scottish national consciousness. Increasingly activities important to the individual have taken place within a Scottish rather than a British framework. There is therefore little need to explain the existence of the Scottish sense of identity. What is interesting is how this has become politically relevant and why, after so many years of failure, the nationalist movement began to achieve success when it did. This book hopes to make a small contribution towards providing a perspective from which the answer to such questions may be more clearly seen.

CHAPTER TWO

Nationalist Movements before 1707

There has been a tendency to consider nationalism in Scotland to be a phenomenon that erupted in the late 1960s or thereabouts and to relate its emergence to particular economic and social conditions existing at that time. But similar economic conditions existed in other parts of the United Kingdom, for example in North East England, which did not lead to any significant political action. Clearly, then, in Scotland nationalism cannot be seen as a consequence of purely economic discontent, and central government policies based on this view are unlikely to be successful. For, as this and the two subsequent chapters are intended to show, modern nationalism is part of a continuing historical process the origins of which are lost in prehistory. An insight into Scottish nationalism can only be gained by understanding both the relationship that has existed through time between England and Scotland, and the different influences that have operated on the two countries to reinforce the feeling of a separate Scottish identity.

The reasons for this are easy to see. Nationalism asserts itself primarily as a reaction to its denial. Scottish nationalism, and the Welsh, Irish, Breton, Basque or Corsican variety for that matter, only exist in strident form as a response to the assimilative tendencies of a larger nation. Those living south of the border frequently believe there is no equivalent English nationalism. This is, of course, an incorrect view, but it is muted in comparison to feelings in Wales, Ireland and Scotland simply because the smaller nations represent no threat to England's separate identity. But this was not always the case. For example, Oliver Cromwell wrote the following at a time when the nations of the British Isles were locked in a violent civil war that crossed national frontiers:

I had rather be overrun by a Cavalierish interest than a Scotch interest, I had rather be overrun by a Scotch interest than an Irish interest ... The quarrel is brought to this state that ... we must be subject to the kingdom of Scotland or the kingdom of Ireland for the bringing in of the King. It should awaken all Englishmen.

And, after the Union of 1707, when Scotsmen were proving their worth in London, there was considerable anti-Scottish feeling in England which sounded at times almost as rabid as the racialism sometimes directed at coloured people in Britain today. Scots were described as 'a plague of locusts', 'mischievous' and 'cold-hearted impudent rogues', which views are a far cry from the sharp but good-natured digs of Dr Johnson. One result of English nationalism at that time, of course, was the difficulty for a Scotsman to forget he was Scots.

For nationalism to exist at all there must be a sense of difference, a sense that there is something in a particular way of life which is distinctive and worth preserving. Frequently the summation of these differences is referred to as 'culture', which is often taken as given and so never to be explained. As was pointed out in Chapter One, culture is difficult to deal with in any simple way. Cultural differences, however, are the net result of historical influences, and the difficulties involved in assessing a culture can be avoided by considering the different historical forces that lead to a feeling of national identity.

If we look at Scottish nationalism from this historical perspective, the type of question we must ask about modern nationalism changes. It is not surprising that nationalism should exist in Scotland – indeed, it has existed for many hundreds of years – but the question is why, at this time, has nationalism become *politically* active instead of, as in the past, restricting itself to literature, the arts, or the sports field, with the exception of a few fringe activists? Nationalism in Scotland is different in kind from the nationalisms of ex-colonial African territories, where the sentiment is fostered to overcome separatist tendencies of tribal loyalties; this often being due to the arbitrary division of the continent by ex-colonial powers. It will be suggested here that at least as far back as Roman times a sense of separate identity has existed in North Britain reinforced by a historical sequence that is different from the English experience. This, together with the type of relationship that existed between Scotland and England, led to the development of nationalism somewhat earlier than was common in Europe.

But, as well as aiding our understanding of the development of nationalism, a historical perspective adds to our understanding of the *context* of nationalism. The past influences the present, partly through inherited social structures and institutions within which we act. However, the past also supplies the myths and aspirations that are now influencing present-day nationalists. The past, or a version of it, lingers on in present consciousness. No nationalist movement achieves real power by sweet reason and logic; also needed are the emotive symbols that link the past with the present. These are often embodied in documents or historic names. The existence of a proven past seems to legitimize the present Movement. If the historical framework is then accepted by a mass-public, an emotional logic is developed that has immense motivational power. Only through the historical context of nationalism does the emotional response become explicable.

Doctrines of geographical determinism are at best only half-truths. Basalt does not breed religion, and the colonization of Iceland was only partly due to a lack of trees from which to build boats. And yet, the more limited the technology of a civilization – technology being the means of environmental control – the greater will be the influence of geographical and climatic factors on forms of social organization. Britain, the largest island in Europe, and yet small in comparison with the Continental land mass, might reasonably have been expected to have developed a homogeneous culture, eventually to become a single nation-state. Instead this tiny isle is inhabited by three collectivities, each claiming separate nationality, incorporated at present somewhat discontentedly into a single state. We should also, perhaps, have expected, if there were to be a division between England and Scotland, that this would fall along the line of the Firths of Forth and Clyde, where the Lowlands begin to give way to more mountainous regions. The placement of the actual border much further south has to be explained by history rather than geography.

It is probable that by the time of the Roman invasion of Britain marked differences already existed between North and South Britons, perhaps due to the different levels of fertility of the land. The Highlands have always been more suitable for grazing than for cultivation, and were not capable of supporting a large population. In addition, it appears that at the time of the invasion the northern tribes were far more united than were those to the south, thus appearing in fact to be a 'United States of Scotland'. Certainly in the field of military operations they presented a far more united front. A primary aim of the Romans in conquering Britain was to provide grain for their Northern European armies, grain which mostly came from the more fertile South Britain. It was not imperative for the Romans to conquer the North providing that they could secure the northern border. And, while they defeated the Caledonians in battle they were not able to retain control of the glens and mountains of the North which were such a different proposition to the gentler lands of the South. So the Romans built two walls to mark the limits of their territorial and military control.

We may assume, then, a difference between the peoples of North and South Britain prior to the Roman invasion, amplified by the long Roman occupation of the South. The Picts in the more northerly parts were largely untouched by Roman culture, while Celtic culture in the South was being eroded by contact with the dominant civilization. And yet, even at this early date, the seeds of the Scottish dilemma were being sown. The area between the two walls was inhabited by Welsh-speaking Britons who, through commerce and trade, were far more Romanized than were their Gaelic-speaking brethren to the north. For centuries this area would be disputed by both North and South and would be settled by Anglo-Saxons, Norsemen, and even later by Norman-French knights. By the time the political boundaries of the future Scottish state had been settled, largely by the middle of the eleventh century, the state had within it a cultural Trojan horse which was far closer culturally to England in both language and custom than to the Celtic Highlands. The Lowlands could be anti-English – perhaps, indeed, they suffered more from the later English incursions than did the Highlands – but the gulf between the Lowlands and the English was not so great as to preclude communication, fairly constant economic interaction, and the development of similar political aims. Until 1745 the struggle between the Highlands and the Lowlands for the soul of Scotland was to continue, to end with the virtual extinction of the Celtic form of social organization, coinciding with the political incorporation of Scotland into a British state. Throughout Scottish history pressures towards cultural assimilation have gone hand-in-hand with drives towards political separatism. The process is not cyclical but continual, and the cultural schizophrenia of Scotland has only been resolved in modern times with the popular acceptance of a mythical Celtic version of Scottish history.

The confused centuries following the departure of the Romans displayed both the assimilative and separatist tendencies in full. While England was largely converted to and inducted into the Roman Church, in Scotland a Church of a different order was instigated by St Columba, which acted to 'strengthen and confirm the Celtic civilization of Picts'. And while this Church was later to come much closer to the Roman Church, up until the Reformation it retained some distinctive elements in terms of language, organization, and religious procedures. Again, while there was considerable pressure both militarily and politically towards integration, the Pictish tribes maintained their independence, perhaps aided by their poverty which provided a poor incentive for either raiders or settlers. In Lothian, however, the Anglo-Saxons did establish settlements, as well as on some of the offshore islands. As one Scottish patriot put it, 'when the Angles came, the acute went North, and the obtuse went South'.

In Northumbria a powerful Saxon kingdom emerged which seemed at one time as if it might unify the whole of North

Britain. But it was not to be. Brude mac Bili, after consolidating his power among the Picts, lured the Northumbrian invaders into injudicious battle and defeated them in AD 685. Thereafter the Pictish kings were free to concentrate on enlarging their kingdoms whenever internecine disputes permitted. While large tracts of England were settled by Vikings who by AD 867 had established a kingdom with York at its centre, in the main the northern kingdom of Alba survived the Viking raids with only a small loss of peripheral territory. Although they settled parts of the Western Lowlands, they made no inroads on the Pictish kingdom itself. Gradually Alba asserted control over the northern rump of the old Northumbrian kingdom, Lothian, thus drawing into itself an alien Anglo-Saxon culture.

The period during and following the Norman Conquest of England was a crucial time in Scottish history. From this time onwards the influence of the dominant Celtic culture began to wane, and that of the more Anglicized Lowlands to prosper. It is doubtful whether Scotland could have withstood the Norman power, but, instead of fighting when William crossed the border in 1072, they recognized his formal overlordship. Even so there were two more invasions from the South in that century. The formal acceptance was aided by the marriage of Malcom Canmore to Margaret, a Saxon princess reared in the courts of Europe. Scotland became part of Christendom, in theory a construct of Christian states, instead of being seen as a rude horde living on the edge of the civilized world. Through the agency of Margaret and her three sons, Scotland began to draw closer to the European form of social organizations, which was feudal; although such changes as did occur were of limited effect in the Highlands where ancient Celtic forms persisted. Celtic society, although hierarchical, was not feudal. The rigid sense of obligation which accompanied landholding in feudal society was not strongly apparent in early Celtic society, where kinship was stressed. David, Margaret's youngest son, who had spent much of his childhood in the English court, planted Norman knights in Lothian and Strathclyde who were loyal to him in the feudal manner. Margaret herself reorganized the Church, encouraging the use of Latin and the growth of the Church as a centre of learning. English became more widely spoken as intercourse across the frontier became more usual, and English law was often adopted or Scottish law adapted to conform to an English model.

Margaret and her progeny carried through what has been called a 'bloodless Norman Conquest' which in the long term had the effect of widening the pre-existing cultural and social division between the Highlands and the Lowlands, symbolized by the use of different languages. Several ineffective attempts were made to resist the tide of assimilation and restore the old Celtic dominance, most notably by Donald Bain, but he was defeated with the aid of Norman arms.

For many years relative peace ensued between England and Scotland, allowing the growth of a prosperity hitherto unknown, while at the same time feudalism took deeper root, both trends being especially evident in the Lowlands. But, after 1286, there followed two hundred and fifty years of intermittent warfare between the two nations, during which time the Auld Alliance was formed between Scotland and France, and Scotland's power and prosperity relative to England declined. Without such an alliance it is doubtful whether Scotland could have withstood the constant English pressure towards unification, for it was the dissipation of English ambition, money, men, and energy in France, often against armies including Scots, that came to Scotland's aid. An interesting parallel, however, may be drawn between 1286 and 1707. In both cases the balance between unity and open division was fine. In the former case union was frustrated by the death of a bride on her way back to Scotland and war resulted, while in the latter case, in spite of great hostility and hatred, union resulted. Had the negotiations in 1706 broken down, war would have been the likely outcome as in 1286. Also, there is clear recognition of the differences between Scotland and England in the terms of the proposed Union of Crowns in 1286. Much as in 1707 Scottish law and customs were to be guaranteed.

It was soon after the failed union of 1286 that two of Scotland's folk-heroes emerged, Wallace and Bruce, who were to serve later nationalists as powerful symbols in the struggle against English oppression. In 1305 Edward I, the Hammer of the Scots, defeated Wallace, took him to England and executed him. After this Edward's overlordship was recognized. In 1306 the Second War of Independence began which resulted in success for the Scots under Bruce at Bannockburn.

What is remarkable about this period in Scotland is the growth of genuine national feeling. At a time when the vision of the ordinary man in much of Europe was limited by parochial boundaries and the neighbouring surrounds, with national honour and prestige the preserve of a small military caste, in Scotland the feeling of nationhood had, in spite of internal divisions, permeated to the heather roots. While nationalism proper is usually considered to have become an important historical force only after the French Revolution of 1789, in Scotland it appears to have been important as early as the fourteenth century. The army of William Wallace, for example, was largely composed of common people, small landholders, the 'community of the land', many of the nobles declining to lend him their support. Possibly this was due to the lighter grip of feudalism in Scotland, both spatially and in intensity, but also because of the historical nature of the North-South division in Britain. A sense of country is again expressed in the Declaration of Arbroath of 1320, in which the case for the recognition of Scotland as a separate entity is put forward:

For, as long as but a hundred of us remain alive, never will we under any conditions be brought under English rule. It is in truth not for glory, nor riches, nor honour that we are fighting, but for freedom – for that alone which no honest man gives up but with life itself.

A strong desire is expressed here, made manifest in battle, for freedom from domination by the South. It is difficult to know now whether this feeling of identity was different from the sentiment motivating later nationalisms, but the effects appear similar. It could have been merely regional, tribal, feudal, or dynastic loyalty, but this seems unlikely. Many historians and social scientists will reserve the term 'nationalism' for the co-lonial or expansionist state, following the establishment of the European bourgeoisie in power, with the ensuing centralization of the State. But in Scotland, with a size small enough in com-parison with her southern neighbour to invite conquest, and yet still large enough to make resistance viable, nationalism was force-fed. The indifferent success of successive invaders prior to the unification of the Scottish state in 1034 provided ideal con-ditions for the emergence of a sense of separate identity, only heightened by English attempts to subsume the Scottish state.

Further, during two-and-a-half centuries of intermittent war-fare Scotland had become exposed to Continental, especially French and German, influences in a way that England had not. England's strength lay in her insularity, while it was in the interests of Scotland to strengthen her ties with Europe as much as possible, this especially being the case prior to the emergence of religious differences amongst the European powers. These contacts affected many aspects of Scottish culture including, for example, a legal system closer to the fundamental law approach than the English system. While Scottish troops fought on French soil against the English, Scottish scholars were to be seen at many of the most famous centres of European learning. St Andrews adopted the curriculum of the University of Paris, and its constitution was derived from other French universities. For a while there was even a French army on Scottish soil, and the Scottish court was at times a centre of French culture.

Up to 1707, in different ways, Scotland was from the time of Edward I under considerable pressure from the South. Respite came only when English strength was sapped by foreign adven-tures, and towards the end of this period by the desire of the English traders to protect their privileges. And, even when peace between the nations did exist, frequently the English would foment internal troubles by supporting one party against another. Although the Scots invaded England and were in turn invaded, there was a qualitative difference between the two acts. It was possible for the Scots to defeat the English on the battlefield, but for the English this did not imply the possibility of permanent subjugation. Yet the defeat of a Scottish army could lead to the permanent conquest of Scotland. The success of Cromwell attests to this. Further, as G. M. Trevelyan notes:

... From the top of the Cheviot ridge the moss-troopers could descry three of the richest shires of Scotland, stretched below them, a helpless prey, while southward they could see nothing but desolate moors. The fertile Lothians and the Tweed Valley could be raided by Percy, but the English midlands could not be touched by Douglas.

The costs of failure were not the same for both sides. The constant aim of England was to integrate Scotland into a Greater England or at least to achieve a dynastic solution through a union of crowns. This was partly due to the personal ambition of monarchs and also because of the desire of England to secure her northern frontiers, thus avoiding the possibility of having to fight a war on two fronts. But in spite of these strong assimilative tendencies the sense of identity persists. The difference is expressed most forcibly in a tract written around 1549:

There is no two nations under the firmament that are more contrary and different from each other than are Englishmen and Scotsmen, albeit that they be within one isle, and neighbours and of one language ... And, to conclude, it is impossible that Scotsmen and Englishmen can remain in concord under one monarch or prince, because their nature and conditions are as different as is the nature of sheep and wolves.

Despite the dissimilarities between the two nations, and the mistrust between them – the result of centuries of mutual violence – union did occur in 1707 after several previous attempts. This had been preceded by a Union of Crowns in 1603, when James VI of Scotland succeeded to the English throne. But this arrangement brought mixed benefits to Scotland. For the first quarter of a century following the Union of Crowns there was comparative peace, partly due to the fact that the king was no longer a counter to be used (or kidnapped) in the struggles between different factions of Scottish noblemen. Backed by the resources of the English state, he was able to achieve a high degree of independence. By 1609 the Borders, 'the Middle Shires' as James called them, had been quieted 'with the assistance of some fathoms of rope', thus allowing some resurgence of prosperity over the devastated battlegrounds. Similarly the Highland chiefs had become less of a direct menace to kingly authority and peace.

On the debit side, however, Scotland lost much by the Union of Crowns in this period, the recognition of which added fuel to the debate which was to occur a century later concerning an alteration to the constitutional arrangement. The removal of the royal court to London cost Edinburgh dear, and much of the monies raised by Scottish noblemen came to be spent in England as they attempted to match the life-style of the English nobility. Their considerable exodus affected the balance of power in Scotland, inclining it a little more towards the emergent commercial classes. By the middle of the seventeenth century, wrote one contemporary:

Our noble families are almost gone. Lennox has little left in Scotland unsold. Hamilton's estate ... is sold. Argyll is no more drowned in debt than in public hatred. The Gordons are gone; the Douglas is little better ... Eglinton and Glencairn are on the point of breaking. Many of our chief families' estates are cracking.

The move by James VI to London, taking the seat of power with him, accelerated the Anglicization of a nobility who, one hundred years later, were to be among the strongest proponents of the Treaty of Union. James has been criticized since for not moving the London court to Edinburgh. But this is unrealistic. At the time England was the more powerful and wealthy nation, and a monarch living away from the centre of power would soon become an irrelevance in important deliberations, especially given the nature of communications at that time. And, in addition, the English crown gave James a great deal more influence internationally than did the Scottish crown, as well as an independent power base both within England and Scotland.

Perhaps in any case, as Edward I suggested, the greater will always draw the lesser, and in terms of wealth, numbers and influence, England was by far the greater.

A further consequence of the Union of Crowns was that Scotland came to be treated as a peripheral region losing, for example, much of her ability to determine defence and foreign policy. In many cases Scottish policy was designed to further the King's English causes, but with few reciprocal benefits for Scotland. James's own attitude to Scotland reinforced this view. After his departure to England he visited Scotland only once before his death for, as he expressed it, he had 'a natural and salmon-like affection to see the place of his breeding'. Apart from this, he was proud of his ability to rule Scotland from London:

This I may say for Scotland, and I may truely vaunt it. Here I sit and govern it with my pen. I write and it is done.

And he hoped that Scotland would

. . . with time become but as Cumberland and Northumberland and those other remote and distant shires.

James desired the Union of Crowns to be closer, as later did William of Orange, but the English Parliament would have nothing to do with it. As an Englishman said during later Union negotiations, 'Scottish Members are like a wooden leg tied to a natural body. Scotland was effectively controlled by the Union of Crowns. They therefore rejected the idea of a free-trade area, for they had little to gain, and also the suggestion that all Scots should in law be considered as naturalized Englishmen. They did, however, agree that Scots born after the accession of James to the English throne should be so treated, while the Scots Parliament drafted a reciprocal Act.

A major factor that aided in bringing the two sides together, albeit by a circuitous route, was religion. If both countries had not been Protestant, any close form of Union would have been very difficult. As it was, the difference between varieties of Protestantism caused enough problems in the civil war. In the seven-

teenth century religion in one of its aspects played very much
the role of political ideologies today, in that it helped to define
the proper relationship between man and the State. Episcopalianism tended to reinforce the status quo and the Divine
Right of Kings: authority was seen as descending from God,
and the king was his secular representative as well as head of the
Church. This happy state of affairs (from the point of view of
the monarch, at least) gave the king control of the pulpit
through patronage, the pulpit being at that time the main means
of ideational control and dissemination in an era of low liter-
acy. Non-conformist religion, on the other hand, either Presbyterianism or Independency, placed the interpretation of proper
conduct, at least in theory, in the hands of the individual, thus
denying the authority of the prelacy and, by extension, the king.
Charles I even attempted to prove that he was the rightful head
of the Church by commissioning a study to prove his descent
from Adam, thus legitimizing his authority. But earlier, when
Melville could claim that there were two kingdoms in Scotland,
each with its separate spheres, and that the king was subject to
his ministers in the same way as other men, he was not merely
stating a theological doctrine but also challenging the existing
power structure. Within both England and Scotland the underlying struggle was against the idea and practice of absolutism
which seemed inappropriate in an age of commercial expansion, and in both cases religion played an important role.

It was the Scots who instigated the civil war. In the Second
Bishops' War they had even invaded England as far as New-
castle. But although a section of the Scottish people, headed by
the Church, had common cause with the English anti-Royalist
faction and fought on the same side, there were differences between the rebelling Scots and their English allies that finally led
to the successful invasion and conquest of Scotland by Cromwell. Firstly, the Church, by means of the 'Army of the Lord',
wished to impose Presbyterianism on England, partly through
religious zeal and partly to protect their own religious revolution. The rejection of Episcopalianism was in small part the
rejection of Anglicization. Also the Scots were not prepared to go

as far as Cromwell in abandoning the monarch. Charles I was a Scottish Stewart king, and his execution caused a great deal of resentment in Scotland. They proclaimed his son king, a situation that Cromwell could not tolerate.

The ensuing enforced union between England and Scotland was, however, moderate in its demands on the Scottish people. Cromwell did not dismantle the Church, although he reduced its civil powers, while certain aspects of the legal system were reformed, as well as the whole of Britain being turned into a free-trade area. In fact, the settlement was not too dissimilar from the 1707 Treaty of Union, the major difference being it was imposed rather than chosen. This fact did not allow the various intra-national interests the freedom to reconcile their differences or encourage the desire to reach a compromise.

Following the collapse of Cromwell's incorporating union after his death, and the repeal of all laws enacted since 1638, the restoration of Charles II also restored the Union of Crowns with the blessing of both countries. The Scots had not enjoyed the higher taxes that union with England had entailed, partially from the need to finance twenty-four military establishments. Although trade had benefited, the English had become jealous of their commercial privileges. Now, as in the time of James VI, Scotland was once again ruled by a distant autocrat. And, to increase Scottish discontent, bishops were restored. The ensuing uprisings that this stimulated were easily suppressed with considerable brutality and with religious persecution following. It seemed as if this was an attempt to assimilate Scottish religion to the English model. But, following the Glorious Revolution of 1688, the Scottish Parliament gained power, in theory at least, equivalent to that of their English counterpart, as well as having the General Assembly of the Kirk restored.

The acceptance of William of Orange as king, however, weakened the Union of Crowns. Firstly the emotional bonds that had tied the Scots to a Stewart monarchy were broken. William could not command the same loyalty or affection and his commands were treated with less reverence. Secondly, the strengthening of Parliament and the restoration of the General

Assembly meant that there were bodies in Scotland capable of making decisions independently of both the king and the English Parliament. The later disputes were due in large measure to the Scots attempting to pursue policies against English interests, which earlier would not have occurred owing to the ability of the king to restrict the scope of Scottish initiative. Responsible government in Scotland implied either that the realms be separated completely, or that they be amalgamated. The king could not ride two horses at once. And one of the factors making for the acceptance of the Union in 1707 was the discovery by the Scots that they were not able to ameliorate Scotland's condition in the face of English intransigence. Before Union was accepted the two nations were again on the brink of war.

Up to 1680 Scotland's material prosperity increased. Trade recovered slowly after the Restoration, interrupted only by the two Anglo-Dutch wars, culminating in the early 1670s with something of a trade boom. From 1680 onwards, however, prosperity began to decline, and after 1690 conditions in Scotland became serious. There were several harvest failures, which led to hunger and popular discontent, while the Anglo-French wars cut Scotland off from her traditional markets, allowing the neutral Scandinavian traders to profit. In addition, tariffs were imposed by England on several Scottish exports.

So, while Scotland grew poorer and was racked by internal dissension, England grew richer and more powerful. The Scots identified the cause of England's prosperity as the colonial trade, since this supplied raw materials, luxuries and markets from which Scotland was largely excluded. There were, of course, many Scots in the English colonies, dispatched there after the 1654 and 1685 risings in Scotland. The Scots, inspired by the strange genius of William Paterson, attempted to break out of this economic straitjacket by founding a colony of their own. They finally decided on Darien, close to where the Panama canal now runs, as the ideal location. Scots had tried at least twice before to found colonies, but with no more success than on this occasion. In 1629, for example, an attempt was made to found a colony, but Charles I had surrendered all the Scottish settlements in 1632. As with Darien, the Scots felt that their interests had been subordinated to those of England. The Darien project, which was a truly national venture, was misconceived and mismanaged from the start. It aroused the hostility of the English Parliament, who saw it as a threat to their own colonial trade and therefore forbade the raising of capital in England. Further, William used his influence to prevent money being raised in Europe and in the event, the venture swallowed up perhaps between a quarter and a half of all the available liquid capital in Scotland, which inhibited development in other directions. In addition, the Spaniards considered Darien to be part of their territory. King William, owing to the delicate political situation in Europe, did not wish to anger the Spaniards and so provided no protection for the hopeful colonists. Indeed, he went further, as this proclamation by the Governor of Jamaica shows:

> In His Majesty's name and by command, strictly to command His Majesty's subjects, whatsoever, that they do not presume, on any pretence whatsoever, to hold any correspondence with the said Scots, not to give them any assistance of arms, ammunition, provisions, or any other necessaries whatsoever . . .

Further, as the Scots soon discovered, the possibilities for trade at Darien were limited, and the mosquito-infested swamps caused widespread fever. By the time the colony was finally abandoned, due to fever, the rigours of sailing, or Spanish guns, the venture had cost some two thousand lives, many ships, and a good deal of Scotland's wealth. Yet Paterson, who went to Darien, lost a wife, and nearly died of fever himself, could still write of the bankrupt company of Scotland:

> This company hath rather been calculated and fitted for and towards bringing a Union than for subsisting in an ununited state . . . no good patriot would have been angry when even the miscarriage of that design hath contributed to the Union.

The Darien failure was traumatic as far as Scottish hopes and aspirations were concerned. There were few families in Scotland who had not suffered either through bereavement or financial loss. And the English were held to blame. Three sailors from an English ship were hanged for crimes they did not commit, symbolizing the prevalent xenophobia. Yet the importance of Darien was that, while it brought to the surface all the traditional fear and dislike of the English, it also convinced an important section of Scottish public opinion that there was no way forward for Scotland outside the context of a closer Union. The alternative was for Scotland to become to an even greater extent a poverty-stricken peripheral backwater region on the edge of Europe. For conditions did not improve. Trade with England more than halved between 1698 and 1706, a trade which was relatively immune from interference due to war. Both before and after Darien dissatisfaction with the Union of Crowns had increased. England, again in dispute with France, desperately needed to secure her northern borders where there existed a hostile nation with a strong Jacobite following, especially in the Highlands. But when negotiations were begun for a closer Union in 1702 the English dragged their heels, unwilling as yet to accept the price of Union. Following the breakdown of negotiations hostility increased in Scotland, where between 1703 and 1704 four Acts were passed which showed the English how serious was the Scottish disaffection. Most importantly the Scots threatened to dissolve the Union of Crowns on the death of Anne, as well as indicating an intent to pursue their own foreign policy rather than that of England. The English Parliament, in turn, passed Acts hostile to the Scots.

For many hundreds of years the English had been attempting to incorporate the Scottish nation, and in the process there had developed a sense of Scottish nationhood based on distinctive cultural differences due in part to the different histories of the two nations. In spite of this, and somewhat paradoxically, at a time when the dislike and distrust of the English had never been greater, the incorporating Treaty of Union was signed and put into effect. Later writers have tried to explain this strange happening, a complete reversal of the position adopted by the Scottish Parliament a few years earlier – composed of the same people – when a rejection of any form of union seemed most likely by means of the dissolution of the Union of Crowns. On the one hand the acceptance of the Treaty was seen as an act of wise statesmanship, while on the other hand it is seen as the result of bribery, corruption, and self-interest. An ex-chairman of the SNP, for example, is quoted as saying:

In 1707 how many ordinary people wanted the Union of the parliaments? None. Nobody asked them. The thing was wangled through by a small group with no mandate from the country at all.

Certainly many of the citizens of Edinburgh did not want the Union, and a commentator at the time expressed the feelings of the rioters thus: 'The people are eagerly disposed to see justice done to these delinquents' (referring to the Scottish Unionists). In addition, one third of the Shires, one quarter of the Burghs, and some Presbyteries and Kirks sent petitions against the Union. Yet, as ever, the reality was far more complex, and any simple assertion of self-interest does not cover the case adequately. A contemporary described the motives for union in this way:

Trade with most, Hanover with some, ease and security with others, together with a general aversion to civil discords, intolerable poverty . . . and constant oppression.

Statements attributing the Union to the corruption of Parliament or to undemocratic procedures ignore the different standards then operative in public life, and attempt to impose on the eighteenth century notions more appropriate to the twentieth. And such activity is not a mere quibble of historical interpretation; it attempts to put the blame for the present state of Scotland on the betraying Unionists. By historical implication, therefore, no true Scot is a unionist. If emotive analogies of this kind are used, then it becomes difficult to debate rationally the real issue as to whether Scotland would benefit from independence.

With the strength and durability of Scottish nationalist feeling, there was also a sense of frustration and political impotence experienced in Scotland. Clearly the Union of Crowns was not a long-term solution to the problems of either England or Scotland. The connection between Scotland and the Crown had grown too tenuous to guarantee Scottish quiescence, from the English point of view. Similarly complete separation was not a viable alternative for either nation, militarily for England, economically for Scotland. The Scottish commissioners did suggest a federal arrangement – perhaps for reasons connected more with public relations rather than with any real hope – but this was not accepted by the English commissioners. They felt it would have given the Scots all the benefit of union in terms of trade, while not solving the security problem as fully as an incorporative union.

To the Scots a full union seemed the only way by which national progress could be achieved. An increase in wealth, commerce and trade was seen as a necessary condition for future Scottish development. There were those who argued for an austerity programme within Scotland to reduce the dependency on foreign trade and to improve the balance of foreign trade. But, in the event, they proved to be in the minority as also were those interests that feared English competition in a free market. To define national progress in terms of trade and commerce is not necessarily a selfish point of view – although it is probably a class-orientated view – but it can equally well be seen as a definition of what was perceived to be the public good. The Treaty of Union was the only way that Scots of the time could see of guaranteeing the future of Scotland, given the current notions of progress. Further, if union had not gone through, there was a possibility of civil war, let alone war with England. The Treaty of Union can be seen, therefore, as an expression of nationalism in dire circumstances, and from a particular point of view that seemed appropriate at that time. There is, of course, no reason to assume that the continuance of this constitutional arrangement is still in Scotland's interest.

Further, the mildness of Cromwell's regime some fifty years earlier had remained in the popular mind, as well as some of the trade benefits flowing from this. A not so distant example of

full union existed. In addition, the Scots had become habit-
uated, however discontentedly, to a degree of control from
London, and it was sensible to hope that by means of full union
they could have more say in policies that affected them instead
of merely reacting to English policy. Also, the Scottish upper
classes had by now a great deal in common with their opposite
numbers in England. There was the similarity of language, increasingly of education, and more importantly, the same view
of progress was current among both groups. Religion, given the
terms of the Treaty, proved to be no problem, whereas even
half a century earlier it would have proved an insuperable barrier to voluntary union. Therefore, while assimilation had occurred, especially in the Lowlands, this did not imply any
lessening of the sense of a separate Scottish identity. At the very
moment of union, indeed, both aspects were displayed in full
and to some degree have been exhibited ever since. It is an
error, therefore, to see the ending of the separate Scottish state
as indicating the end of the sense of nation, as recent events
confirm. Nationalism is not dependent upon statehood for its
existence. Rather, the loss of political independence was merely
the price that had to be paid at that time to ensure continuing
national development, a price that appears to some to have
been too high.

The Act of Union guaranteed the retention of three Scottish
institutions: the mint, the legal system, and the Church. The
Union gave Scotland 45 members in the House of Commons, as
against 513 English and Welsh members, with 16 Scottish
peers to join the 190 English peers. While in today's terms the
number of representatives seems grossly inadequate – the population proportions being only five-to-one in favour of England –
by eighteenth-century standards the settlement was quite gener-
ous. The prevailing theory was that property rather than people
should be represented, for only those with a 'stake in the country'
were considered to be responsible enough to vote. In terms of
wealth Scotland was grossly over-represented, for England was
thirty-six times more wealthy. In addition an 'Equivalent' was
paid, to be used to benefit Scottish industry and to reimburse

those who had invested in the Darien venture. The Union had one further consequence which is interesting to note. As from its acceptance both England and Scotland ceased to exist in law, but were joined in the state of Britain. This meant, of course, that when 'infringements' of the Act occurred, absolutely nothing could be done legally to right the case since both parties had ceased to exist as legal entities. And, just as there was no body with the right to appeal against infringements, so there was no body charged with the duty of supervising the proper application of the terms of the Act. It may be the case that it is impossible to infringe the Act of Union, since it was not an Act of the Parliament of Britain. But what may or may not be the case in law, on many occasions Scots have cited the Act of Union when they have considered its provision breached by various Acts of Parliament. And, as a centre for argument it has been capable of generating considerable emotional heat up to the present day.

CHAPTER THREE

From the Union to the First World War

The traditional orthodoxy, accepted even by some Scottish nationalist writers, is that nationalism after the Union can be divided into three periods. From 1707 to 1750 there was unrest, followed by quiescence and acceptance until the middle of the nineteenth century, since when there has been constant nationalist agitation. This picture, however, over-simplifies a complex reality. While in the first period considerable discontent took place, not all the instances can be considered nationalistic in origin. Undoubtedly, as in the case of the armed insurrections of this time, there were nationalistic elements, and the consequences of successful uprising would have affected the constitutional arrangements between Scotland and England. Nevertheless, the prime factors were not nationalistic but dynastic, religious and cultural.

In the second period we can again find numerous examples of nationalism, expressed in the claim either to a separate identity or to new constitutional arrangements, but these were essentially an adjunct of other social movements, especially radicalism. Nationalism as a 'pure' political interest only really becomes evident after the First World War. What, however, is important during this second period is that the various radical organizations that arose in Scotland, although in general part of a British phenomenon, did have separate organizations even though there were linkages with both English and Irish radical movements. The existence of a distinctive organization becomes very important in the complex situation after 1920. We should further note that during the third period, from 1853 onwards until comparatively recently, nationalist demands were far milder than the expressions of the modern Movement. In general, federalism was the most extreme alternative considered. Only after the decline of John MacCormick's Scottish Covenant Association in 1954 did the call for separation begin to dominate.

The Union aroused considerable discontent at both the popular and elite levels. In 1708 the French attempted to land 6,000 men in Scotland in support of the Jacobite cause. Bad navigation and an efficient British fleet prevented this landing, but it is probable that, had the landing occurred, there would have been considerable popular support for it, more so than in 1715 or 1745. And, because of the military weakness of the Government at that time, a successful invasion would have been a strong possibility.

Even without armed insurrection the years following 1707 seemed to indicate, even to those who had supported it, that the Union had failed. The English attitude tended to aggravate the latent hostility between the two nations. It was patronizing, even sometimes abusive, and the Government sometimes displayed an amazing lack of any kind of political tact. Perhaps this was due to difficulties in communication, but also because the affairs of Scotland were conducted by a small aristocratic elite, often Anglicized, and in search of patronage. As early as 1710 the House of Lords chose to reverse a Scottish judicial decision, overruling the terms of the Act of Union in both its religious and legal guarantees. Further, the efficiency of the tax-gathering machinery became greater, which led to discontent. The woollen industry in Scotland suffered badly from English competition and increased salt tax affected the herring industry. In addition, the Government attempted to levy a malt tax, but heavy Scottish opposition led to its withdrawal (although it was imposed successfully in 1725). It is not surprising that, with the first effects of the Union appearing so unhappy, an attempt should be made to rescind it. This occurred in 1713, when a motion was introduced into the House of Lords to this effect, was supported by all the Scottish members, and was only narrowly defeated. The Union was hardly more appealing to the English, but, as the Speaker said, England 'had catcht Scotland and would keep her fast'.

The second attempt to change the constitutional order by force occurred in 1715. In part the failure can be attributed, as was the failure of the '45, to the inability of the Stewart kings to conform to the Presbyterian Lowland wishes. In both 1715 and 1745, the majority of the fighting men came from the Highlands, the stronghold of Catholicism and Episcopalianism, which did not in the main endear the Highlanders to the Lowlanders. To wish to break the Union was one thing; but to espouse the Roman cause was quite another. Both of these insurrections, whilst being Scottish in origin, were also internecine disputes rather than expressions of nationalism. And the result of these military ventures was to confirm the death of the Celtic order in Scotland. While the measures adopted after the 1715 uprising were fairly mild, after the 1745 rebellion there was extremely harsh repression. The measures taken then attacked the Celtic System at the top by removing from clan chiefs their 'hereditary jurisdictions'. again in violation of the Act of Union but now with the support of many Lowlanders. The clansmen were disarmed and the symbols of clanship, such as the wearing of the kilt, forbidden. And, where estates were not forfeited, the effect of the legislation was to change completely the status and function of the Highland Chief. No longer was his position measured by the number of men he could call to arms, but instead he moved closer to being the southern type of landlord.

It is probable that the 'modernization' of Highland society was merely accelerated by the events following Culloden, rather than being caused by them. Highland society was already under a direct cultural attack more insidious, prolonged and effective than mere military conquest could offer, and again the stimulus for this action was in the main religious. In 1709 the Society for the Propagation of Christian Knowledge started setting up schools in the Highlands. By 1732 there were schools already established in 109 parishes. Further, the teaching was conducted in English rather than Gaelic; it was not until 1758 that any religious texts were available in Gaelic and not until many years later that a full Gaelic Bible was used. The Lowland Presbyterians had a detestation of the 'Irish' language of the North which served, in their view, to insulate the barbaric Highlander from both religion and progress. Perhaps, though, the cultural attack on the Highlands did ease the passage of Highlanders from the North, both to other countries and to the developing industries of the Lowlands. They had at least some familiarity with English which gave them more flexibility than they would have had otherwise.

The decline of Celtic culture would not be important in a work about nationalism if it were not for the fact that today it is the myth of a Celtic Scottish past that serves as the popular historical perspective of many Scots. The past has an emotional logic which acts to bind together events and people who in reality had a few, if any, links. With the acceptance of Celtic mythology, Scottish history is seen as a single broad path leading straight to the present, a perspective which aids greatly the interpretation of current events. Wallace, Bannockburn, Culloden and Burns in combination have an effect that no amount of learned exposition could achieve, and seen as part of a common, unique and shared heritage, they are that much more persuasive. The inaccuracy of historical perception is irrelevant to its effectiveness in generating myths.

Scotland was culturally divided for most of its history as a nation-state, with the aggressive Lowland culture eventually achieving dominance after Culloden. A sign of this is the virtual eclipse of Gaelic as a language of daily intercourse for all but a very few Scots. Then, following the proscription of all things Celtic in 1746, a curious transformation occurred, strongly aided by Sir Walter Scott among others. His poems and novels ennobled the Highlander, emphasizing the virtues and romance of the hardy life-style which had by then reached a point of decay rendering its revival highly improbable. Even comparatively recent conflicts became, in this historical and romantic light, swathed in the mists of nostalgia. By 1822, when the royal court appeared in Edinburgh in kilts, the major battle was over. In the popular mind the Scots had a common past, a history and a heritage which all could share, sufficiently colour-

ful and distinctive to ensure the symbols of Scotland international recognition. These symbols of the past, pre-eminent
among them kilt, bagpipes, thistle, whisky and clan, were things
to be proud of, differentiating the Scots lion from the English
bulldog. This historical mutation reaffirmed the identity of
Scotland as a unique entity in spite of the Union and provided a
past to which all Scots could relate. The almost universal ac-
ceptability of this version of history perhaps goes a long way to
explaining the classless nature of Scottish nationalism. In the
early phases of modern nationalism – from 1850 onwards –
different classes tended to display their nationalism in separate
organizations. Latterly, however, the nationalist movement has
drawn members exactly proportionally from all classes.

Nationalism was not prominent in Scottish political life between 1750 and 1850. The reason usually given for this quiescence is that the attention of the nation was directed elsewhere,
which is partially true. Scotland was developing economically
and industrially at a tremendous pace, and at the same time
there was an intellectual and cultural explosion that made Edinburgh one of the foremost cities in Europe. Records show that
between 1728 and 1760 linen output increased five-fold; there
were sixty-seven Glasgow-owned ships in 1735 while by 1776
there were 386; tobacco imports between 1724 and 1771 increased ten-fold, while between 1723 and 1800 the number of
animals sold increased three-fold and the average weight per
animal doubled. And, in the midst of this economic and industrial progress, Adam Smith and David Hume were changing the
direction of Western thought. While in the arts, history, literature
and philosophy there was an unprecedented outburst of genius.
The benefits of Union were seen to have been achieved and in
most of prosperous Scotland it was now rarely questioned. In
terms of national development, since the Union, Scotland had
joined the leaders of Europe in many fields.

Yet, the idea that energy previously invested in nationalist
politics was now taken up with more global issues is only partially correct. Three further factors must be taken into account.
Firstly, the organization of the Scottish political system was

such that it did not reflect the popular mind, but only a very small section of Scottish society. Secondly, during this period, partly because of the nature of the electoral system, nationalism rode on the back of radicalism. Thirdly, it was only towards the end of this period that de facto freedom became affected by the centralizing of Government, leading to a reaction that demanded greater Scottish control of Scottish affairs.

Voting in Scotland was in the eighteenth century very much a minority affair. As such, the system tended to promote the interests of a very small class of people. For example, in 1788 there were only 2,624 Scottish voters, while in Cromarty the Member of Parliament was elected on only six votes. Since the right to vote was on the basis of property qualification, the voting public was very unrepresentative and what nationalistic feeling did exist tended to be expressed outside Parliament. From the Union until 1850 Scottish Members voted as a bloc in Parliament only three times. For the rest of the time their actions were in the main indistinguishable from the English Members. Until 1746 there was a Scottish Secretary who, with the Lord Advocate, acted as a minister with special responsibility for Scotland. The secretaryship was abolished following the 1745 rising. In 1828 the Home Secretary was given responsibility for Scotland, advised by the Lord Advocate. It was not until 1885 that the post of Scottish Secretary was restored, and then only after considerable political agitation. Therefore, for a long time the means of influencing the London Government was limited firstly by the nature of the electoral system and secondly by the fact that there were few channels other than outright petition through which popular demands could be made in Parliament. Seen from London, the dream of James I was being fulfilled, and for a while Scotland was even termed 'North Britain'. The use of Parliament as a means of political protest by Scottish patriots was not generally possible before the electoral reforms of 1832, and even then only got into full swing during the latter half of the century.

While the main expression of nationalism during this period was by radical groups, it did occur elsewhere, even in Parliament, but to a very much more limited extent. In literature, for example, Macpherson, Burns and Scott were fierce patriots, although Unionists. In 1762 the Poker Club was formed 'to stir up the fire and spirit of the nation', with the aim of agitating for a complete reform of the Unionist political system existing in Scotland. Two further examples of Scottish dissent occurred in 1785 and 1825, this time against proposed Government legislation. On the first occasion Dundas attempted to reduce the size of the Court of Session, with the laudable aim of making it more efficient. But the 'obvious utility' of the measure was not apparent to all Scotsmen. The Scots Members voted against the bill, which was withdrawn, but not until there had been a considerable outcry against the measure. A letter in the *Edinburgh Evening Consort*, for example, made the point:

It is not improbable that this bill is brought into Parliament to try if the people of Scotland will submit to having the Articles of Union broke; and the next thing will be to break through them with regard to land tax, etc. America would not consent to being taxed without its own consent.

Clearly, the election of a representative did not imply, to this writer, the automatic acceptance of legislative decisions. Scotland was seen as having interests quite separate from those of England unprotected by mere Parliamentary representation. In 1825, in order to deal with a domestic banking crisis, Parliament proposed to ban the issue of bank notes up to the value of five pounds, which represented some 63 per cent of Scottish currency. Not unnaturally this led to a great deal of discontent with nearly five hundred Scottish petitions being made to Parliament. The main complaint then, and echoed today by nationalists of all complexions, is that measures taken to remedy English problems are frequently not applicable to Scotland and may be actually injurious. A major impetus to union was the inability of the monarchy to ride two horses at once pulling in different directions. A century later Scotland as a separate entity was, by some people, perceived to have interests of her own. The British identity, at a time when nationalist demands were comparatively quiet, had not eradicated the Scottish mentality altogether.

Towards the end of the eighteenth century the radical movements in Scotland took on a nationalist tinge, although their major aim was still to reform the political system. The Friends of the People, which began in Scotland in 1792, leaned more towards Paine and Rousseau than to any outright nationalism. As with later radical groups that embraced nationalism, it was primarily seen as a means of attaining their chief ends. Indeed, many of the pamphlets of the Friends of the People speak of 'Britons' rather than 'Scots'. While the material progress of Scotland had brought prosperity to many people, the industrial revolution in Scotland as in England also led to the formation of a large disadvantaged population. There was a deprived mass for radical movements to draw upon, especially among the declining traditional industries. At a time when grain and oatmeal prices were fluctuating wildly weavers' wages, for example, were declining, as was their status in the hierarchy of craftsmen. In 1792 the Friends of the People were strong enough to call a National Convention at which about eighty branches were represented. A letter in 1793, reporting the state of Scottish opinion and noting the different treatment accorded to Scottish and English radicals, states:

... it requires more confidence in the good sense of our countrymen than I can reasonably have not to believe that it is possible (though I do not think probable) that a fatal national jealousy may arise. Scotland has long groaned under the chains of England and knows that its connection there is the cause of its greatest misfortunes ...

Another letter, this time to Home Secretary Dundas, following the riots after the Militia Act, expressed fears that the Union was in danger and that 'the fate of Scotland hung upon our measures'. Later, the Report of the Committee of Secrecy in 1799 alleged that the United Scotsmen, with their English and Irish allies, had separatist aims to found 'on the ruins of established government' three republics in the British Isles. The severity of the repression used by Central Government, which included executions and deportations, was not entirely without cause. France was again challenging Britain, and French frigates were seen off the Scottish coast. Further, the French Revolution struck sympathetic chords in many Scottish minds; in both England and Scotland mild agitation for reform was not distinguished by the ruling class from revolutionary intent. As radicalism was generally stronger in Scotland, so repression was heavier.

In 1820 there was again radical agitation in Scotland, centred this time on Glasgow. It included the posting of a 'Proclamation of the Provisional Government'. While this was probably the work of a Government agent – the document makes reference to Magna Carta rather than the Declaration of Arbroath which would be more normal for Scottish patriots – the fact that it was framed in separatist terms is itself significant. An inflammatory statement with little popular appeal would not be effective in drawing dissidents into the open. Hence it can be inferred that among the Glasgow insurrectionists there was considerable sympathy for the establishment of a Scottish Government.

Chartism in Scotland, like other radical movements, with the possible exception of the United Scotsmen, was nationalistic only in a low key. But again, that it was both a popular movement and had a nationalist aspect is itself significant. The *Scottish Vindicator*, a Chartist paper, intended to devote much of its space to the speeches of patriots, especially those who had suffered in the people's cause in 1793–4, 1819–20 and 1839. In 1844 the Birmingham Quaker Joseph Sturge went to Glasgow to address a Chartist meeting after having lost his following in England, but retaining and increasing his Scottish following. His main interest was to reform Parliament and, especially, to introduce universal suffrage. But, after the achievement of this end, federalism should be the next step with local parliaments sitting in Ireland and Scotland. 'It was ridiculous,' he said, 'that they (in Scotland) should be compelled to go to London for everything that concerned them locally.' While none of the Chartists were prominent in the Nationalist Association, formed in 1853, the membership being drawn from different social classes, yet by voicing similar protests for several years they prepared the way for the later more influential movements.

But for the long-term development of nationalism the separatist views and aims of the radical movements were probably less important than the fact that they saw themselves as acting in a Scottish context. While most Scottish radical groups had links with English and Irish movements, yet they maintained a separate organizational existence even when preaching a text of internationalism. The Act of Union guaranteed the Law, the Church and the mint. But initially with the extra-parliamentary radical movements, and later with the organization of mass parties, Scotland provided herself with a form of political machinery capable of articulating a separate Scottish interest. Following the extension of suffrage and the development of an increasingly open political system, when the Scottish sections of the British political parties failed to state the Scottish interest – for example, prior to 1886 and after the First World War – a well-established precedent existed for extra-parliamentary expression. In part this was also influenced by the nature of the Scottish Church, the General Assembly of which was not averse to making statements with a strong political content. As the nineteenth century progressed, the Scottish point of view was increasingly seen as being different from the British interest, and if not expressed in Parliament, it would be proclaimed elsewhere.

It is no accident, then, that some of the most ardent nationalists have been ministers in one or other of the Scottish Churches. In 1850, for example, only a few years after the Disruption, the Reverend James Begg, wishing to stimulate a national revival, issued a pamphlet that was influential in the formation of the National Association for the Vindication of Scottish Rights. Again, it was the Reverend James Barr who was one of the most persistent activists in Parliament in the cause of home rule for Scotland as Member of Parliament for Motherwell after the First World War. And, as has been noted before, in the absence of a Parliament in Scotland the General

Assembly took on some of its functions and acted as a forum for public debate. The Disruption of 1843, while primarily a matter of religious conscience, had both political and nationalistic undertones. The argument was as old as Protestantism in Scotland, the seceding minority declaring that a British Parliament could not legislate on Scottish religious matters. It was the same argument that had been pursued by Knox and Melville regarding the respective spheres of influence of Church and State. But on this occasion the importance from a nationalist point of view was that the dissenters grounded part of their case in the Act of Union. The consent of the Scottish nation was necessary to authorize changes in religious affairs, and the will of the British Parliament was patently not the same as the will of the Scottish people.

By the middle of the nineteenth century new conditions had emerged· which were conducive to the rise of organizations more explicitly nationalistic. In particular, the improvement of communications and the increased degree of government intervention meant that Scottish affairs obtruded more into Westminster politics. There had always been some interest, but three-week-old events tended to lack the impact of three-day-old news. And the political news from London was now of more importance to Scots, for gradually in Scotland, as in England, the policy of *laissez-faire* was breaking down in practice, although in theory it was still operable.

This meant that in many fields of social policy Central Government was legislating on matters which previously had been dealt with at the local level – factory conditions, the state of the poor, provision of asylums, for example, all came under governmental scrutiny. While this undoubtedly led, at least in the long term, to an improvement in social conditions, it also led to a decrease in the degree of control that Scots felt they had over their own affairs. In many areas of life the existence of a London government was unimportant or only peripheral to Scottish local control, but gradually this de facto freedom was being eroded. There came a reaction but this time from the more articulate and prosperous sections of society where pleas for more Scottish control of Scottish affairs were less likely to be rejected as dangerous or radical. Linked to the argument about Scottish control of Scottish affairs – which was argued on the grounds that an English-dominated Parliament could not legislate efficiently for a country of whose conditions they were ignorant – was the question of Parliamentary congestion and the Irish question. An argument for some kind of legislative devolution was the fact that the Imperial Parliament was becoming overloaded and congested with legislation they had no time to scrutinize properly. For some English Parliamentarians this was the major point in favour of devolution. But it should also be noted that by today's standards the demands of the nationalists between 1850 and 1914 were very moderate. In the main they demanded the restoration of the Scottish Secretary, an increase in the number of Scottish representatives in Parliament, both of which were met by 1886, and thereafter a demand for a federal system in the United Kingdom. At no time was separation or independence an aim of the major activists, although there were a few fringe nationalists for whom this was an end.

In 1852 James Grant, an Edinburgh author, wrote of the way that England had broken the terms of the Union. He wanted more Scottish representatives at Westminster, to give Scotland a larger voice, and the restoration of the Scottish Secretaryship which had lapsed in 1746. In addition, he claimed that England was getting more out of the Union in financial terms, that the revenue raised by the Government in Scotland was less than the amount of public spending there. At the time Grant was probably correct, but it is interesting to note that nationalists since that time have repeatedly made the same point though probably with less and less justification. But as an emotive debating point it has a considerable effect which remains after the welter of esoteric statistics and counter-statistics has abated. Between 1845 and 1865, however, Scotland was producing about one-quarter of Britain's pig-iron; by 1910 one-third of all Britain's steel ships were built on the Clyde; while by the turn of the century the industrial output of Scotland was one-seventh that

of England and Wales combined. So it seems probable that
Grant was right, a point tacitly admitted when the Goschen
Formula, upon which regional government expenditure was
based, was introduced in 1888.

As well as the more normal pamphleteering means of persuasion, Grant aroused the interests of the Scottish public by his
campaign against the irregularities in the Royal Arms. Such
symbolic protests have played an important part in nationalism,
not because of any effect they may have had on Government,
but because of the interest and sympathy they arouse in Scotland. Theodore Napier's petition against the misuse of Scottish
names, John MacCormick's court case about the proper title of
the Queen, Wendy Wood's hoisting of the Scottish flag at Stirling Castle, and the removal of the Stone of Destiny from Westminster Abbey fall into the same category. The fact that these
exploits did arouse great public feeling indicates how close to
the surface nationalism has always been.

In 1853 the National Association for the Vindication of
Scottish Rights was formed. The National Association, unlike
the individual nationalists of the past or the radical organizations, carried some weight. It managed to mobilize a comparatively large section of Scottish opinion, especially in
Conservative and Liberal quarters, even though it was officially
non-party. The Reverend James Begg, James Grant, W. E.
Aytoun and Duncan McLaren, the Scottish Liberal leader, were
among the founder members. In November a public meeting
was called in Edinburgh. It was supported not only by private
members but also by some town councils and the Convention of
Royal Burghs. The meeting passed five resolutions, against the
subverting of Scottish institutions under the pretence of centralizing the economy, for increased representation in Parliament, and for the restoration of the office of Secretary for
Scotland. A meeting held the following month in Glasgow, and
attended by five thousand people, asked for a separate Scottish
Assembly for the direction of those matters which are exclu-
sively Scottish. The 1853 movement, in spite of showing a body
of support for the cause, soon died. To some extent any organ-

ization with national aims at that time had to overcome the stigma of being automatically put in the same category as the Irish. The National Association provoked considerable opposition from the Establishment – they were called 'repealers' and their nationalism an 'anachronism'. More importantly, they failed to develop any grass-roots organization, and neither did the established political parties heed their call. They were, in any event, pushed into the background by the Crimean War.

In 1886 the Scottish Home Rule Association was founded, but prior to this agitation had not ceased, although it was fairly low key and came from the political establishment. By 1885 the issue of representation was settled, firstly by increasing the number of Scottish representatives to sixty in 1863, and then to seventy-two in 1885. In 1869 a number of Scottish Members of Parliament had sent a letter to Gladstone pointing out that much of Scottish legislation was beyond the competence of the Lord Advocate, who was primarily a legal officer, and requesting the formation of a second official post for Scottish business. Gladstone set up a Royal Commission to examine the matter which recommended very much what the Scottish Members had requested. However, neither Gladstone nor Disraeli followed up the report with action. In 1877 a Scottish Member of Parliament suggested that a 'tribunal' should be set up in Edinburgh to consider Scottish private legislation which, owing to the congested Parliamentary timetable, was unduly delayed. It was argued then that if some action were not taken, demands in Scotland would become more extreme. The question of the Scottish Secretary was again raised in 1881, this time in the House of Lords. In 1881, finally, an Under-Secretary was appointed to advise the Home Secretary, the post being filled in the first place by a future Prime Minister, Lord Rosebery. He resigned soon after, since he felt that his power to achieve anything worthwhile was so limited that there was little point in continuing. But he did manage to convince Gladstone, who by this time was in any case very much in favour of devolution, that the creation of a full Secretary for Scotland was desirable. In 1884 there was a large demonstration in Edinburgh under the auspices of the Convention of Royal Burghs to remind London of Scottish feeling on the matter. In 1885 the post of Secretary for Scotland was created.

By 1885 Gladstone was fully converted to Home Rule for both Ireland and Scotland, although a greater degree of devolution was envisaged for Ireland than for Scotland. The case for Scottish devolution was at the same time aided and hindered by the Irish Question. The constant militancy of the Irish representatives at Westminster, and the periodic violence which occurred in Ireland, kept the question of nationalism to the front. And there was a historical linkage between the Irish and Scottish home-rule agitators in that they tended to support each other in their pamphlets and papers and sometimes exchanged speakers. The relationship was not too dissimilar to the type of relationship between Welsh and Scottish nationalism today. Direct Irish influence, however, tended to be much less in the Establishment-dominated devolutionary movements. On the other hand the extremism of the Irish home-rule activists tended to alienate potential home-rule support in Scotland.

Violence had infringed on Scottish nationalist activities only very occasionally, and then only due to extremists outside the main Movement. Indeed, at various times in its history, for example around 1902 with the Young Scots Society, and in the middle 1930s with the SNP, pacifism has been a strong element in Scottish Nationalism. A further hindrance provided by the Irish was that due to their militancy the question of Irish home rule had precedence in all discussions on the subject. Serious discussion in Scotland became constantly deferred until the time that the political party committed to home rule, the Liberals, were no longer in a position to do anything about it. The home-rule activists in Scotland, however, were caught in a dilemma. If they escalated their activism beyond accepted political norms they alienated potential support, but if they agitated along established channels their cause was treated as a secondary problem.

In a document published by the SHRA against the denial or delay of home rule in 1890, the frustration felt due to the Irish situation is clearly reflected. The Association argued that failure to treat Scotland on an equal basis with Ireland 'appears to set a premium upon disorder', and that the claims of Scotland should be dealt with first since Scotland up to 1707 had a Parliament, while the Irish never had a Parliament prior to their incorporation. At a meeting in Edinburgh as late as 1913, the Secretary for Scotland, T. Mckinnon Wood, informed the audience that he was authorized to announce that the Liberal Government had decided to introduce a Scottish self-government bill. But this statement was qualified by Asquith, the Prime Minister, who shortly before, on the introduction of the Government of Ireland bills, said that the bill was 'only the first step in a larger and more comprehensive policy'. Ireland still had to come first. Winston Churchill, at Dundee in 1911, made the point that 'There is nothing which conflicts with the integration of the United Kingdom in the setting up of a Scottish Parliament for the discharge of Scottish business.' But he went on to say that a complete federal system in the United Kingdom would be difficult to achieve, since English internal party politics could not easily be separated from imperial politics. Thus, what to do about England, with her vast numerical preponderance, was an additional problem.

The SHRA was in the main a Liberal organization, and although nominally all-party, it tended to act as a ginger group within the Liberal Party. It had, however, fairly close ties with the emerging Labour movement. As has been pointed out there had been in Scotland considerable sympathy in radical circles for home rule, and this linkage was maintained. Ramsay MacDonald, who later disappointed nationalists just as much as he did socialists, was at one time Secretary to the London branch of the SHRA. Keir Hardie, who from a mining background was instrumental in founding the Scottish Labour Party and later the Independent Labour Party, was an early vice-president of the SHRA. R. B. Cunninghame-Graham, who as a leading radical had stood as a parliamentary candidate, was to become the first president of the National Party of Scotland in 1928.

But, given the prevailing climate of opinion especially after

Gladstone's conversion, the attempt was made to work through the existing parties, more or less as a pressure group, with the aim of mobilizing all shades of political opinion on the nationalist issue. This appeared at the time to be a sensible policy, for by 1912 it seemed to be only a matter of time before some measure of home rule would be granted. The all-party approach was weakened, however, by the split in Liberal ranks following the 1886 General Election, after which the question of home rule became very much a matter of party politics. The Conservatives, in the main, rejected any form of legislative devolution, Balfour stating in 1895 that: 'We object to Home Rule, whether it begins with Ireland and ends with Wales, or begins with Wales and ends with Ireland. We object to the whole thing.' Nevertheless, the all-party approach was not a total failure, and to the extent that it did fail it did not seem to matter very much. Given the seemingly powerful position of the Liberal Party, as one of the two major established parties, it seemed that home rule would still occur. Between 1889 and 1914 Scottish home rule, in a variety of guises, was debated fifteen times in Parliament, including the introduction of four bills. In 1913 a Home Rule bill passed the second reading. In every case after 1893 when home rule was debated a majority of the Scottish Members voting were in favour. In the 1913 debate on the second reading there were forty-five Scottish members for the bill and only eight against. Clearly the Scottish political establishment was both more in favour and less divided about home rule then than is today's Establishment.

The devolution schemes introduced into Parliament varied considerably. At one end of a continuum it was suggested that the Scottish Members of Parliament should sit separately in Scotland in the autumn to consider Scottish legislation. At the other end was the view that full federation was the only viable long-term solution. But independence was not a serious political position, and those suggesting it were relegated to the lunatic fringe. There were, however, some genuine responses to Scottish demands, demands often accompanied by complaints which put English parliamentarians in an awkward position. On the one hand, if they attempted special legislation for Scotland the English were accused of legislating in ignorance of the peculiar conditions affecting Scotland, but if they left it to the Scots they were accused of neglect and disinterest in Scottish affairs. An attempt was made in 1895 to resolve the dilemma by setting up a Scottish Grand Committee with powers to discuss Scottish legislation but not to pass or reject legislation. This committee did not meet after 1895, but in 1907 a Standing Committee on Scottish Bills was constituted to discuss the details and amendments of Scottish legislation, and is still referred to as the Scottish Grand Committee.

None the less, it should perhaps be noted in passing that Scottish home rule was very low on the list of parliamentary priorities before 1912, and generally very little interest was displayed by parliament. Looking back and abstracting particular political incidents both within and outside Parliament over a long period of time gives the impression that Scottish home rule was a constant Parliamentary and social preoccupation, but this was far from being the case. The number of people involved in any home-rule activity was very small at any one time, although steadily increasing as the First World War approached. By 1914 the Young Scots Society claimed to have fifty-eight branches. Within Parliament home-rule debates were rarely attended by more than half the Members and on several occasions the House was counted out, there being insufficient numbers in attendance to continue the debate.

The SHRA, which by its propaganda outside and influence inside Parliament had done much to influence opinion, by the late 1890s had begun to fade. Partly it was a victim of its own success. The Liberal Party were committed to home rule and were merely awaiting the auspicious conjunction of parliamentary power and available time. It seemed that there was little point in continuing to pressure a committed party since a possible result of any excess in this direction, which was possible given the emotive nature of the subject, would be to alienate favourable opinion. In addition, the leadership group had become dispersed, some into Parliament, a number of the radical leaders becoming active in English radical politics; others had just grown old in service. The Young Scots Society was motivated in part by the desire not to let the home-rule issue grow cold through the decline of the SHRA. While the SHRA had been colonized by the Liberal Party only to a degree, the group which took over their role as propagandists for home rule was almost entirely a Liberal organization prior to the First World War, although on the radical wing of the party. The Young Scots Society was formed in 1900 with the aim of defending free speech, and displayed a strong sympathy with the Boer cause. With the ending of the Boer War the Society became more involved in the home-rule cause, making it an important part of their more general programme, which was:

> To stir interest in progressive politics, to encourage the study of history, social and industrial science, to promote Liberal principles; to further the interests of Scotland and to secure for Scotland the right of self-government.

The YSS was very successful as a Liberal ginger group. A great many public meetings were held and in 1912 the Scottish Home Rule Council was formed by the YSS, the Scottish Liberal Association, and the Liberal Members of Parliament. Evidence for their success, and the success of the home-rule movement as a whole can be adduced from the fact that, had the First World War not occurred when it did, Scottish home rule would probably have soon become a fact. But the War changed attitudes, and after it home rule seemed to many people less important. This was partly due to the sense of unity and purpose engendered by the War, when domestic divisions were pushed aside to achieve a single-minded war effort. But also, the major efforts of the various home-rule groups had been channelled through the Liberal Party and, with its collapse as a party capable of forming a majority government, hopes for the speedy introduction of home rule fell. Further, the emergence of the Labour Party as a strong electoral force restructured the dimensions of political debate. Politics was now articulated in terms of class rather than region or nation, this especially being the case after the settlement of the Irish question. The national or regional dimension was seen by many as an irrelevance, even though deference to the Scottish interest was still displayed by parliamentary candidates on election platforms. The final abandonment of the all-party approach by the Young Scots Society also meant that post-war, with the decline in Liberal strength, there were no strong links between the nationalist interest in Scotland and potential support in Parliament. In other words, the nationalists had to begin all over again, only this time in a more hostile environment. The post-war self-government bills had little chance of success, and it was this fact that stimulated the formation of a separate nationalist political party in 1928.

CHAPTER FOUR

The Foundations of Modern Nationalism

Following the First World War the changed political situation in Britain enforced a change in the strategy of nationalist activity. The Liberal Party, upon whom nationalist hopes had been pinned in the immediate pre-war era, was in decline and unable to implement a devolutionary programme. After the Second World War the nationalist movement had therefore to be rebuilt on a different basis.

At first the collapse of the Liberal Party did not seem to matter too much, for there was some Conservative support and a great deal of left-wing sympathy for nationalism in Scotland. While ostensibly the revived SHRA was an all-party body, in reality its major strength emanated from socialist circles. To some extent the nationalist movement post-war attempted to get the same sort of relationship with the Labour movement as it had enjoyed pre-war with the Liberal Party. Labour and Liberal MPs cooperated to some degree over the home-rule issue as, for example, when a National Committee was set up in 1918 to extend the Irish Home Rule legislation to Scotland. The Liberals made attempts to recapture the home-rule movement, but they could no longer hope to deliver the goods and their influence in nationalist circles waned.

Socialist support was particularly apparent between 1918 and 1920. Backing for the SHRA came from the STUC, the ILP, the Cooperative movement and radical and Labour organizations generally. In 1916 the STUC passed a resolution in favour of home rule and in 1917 sent a deputation to the Prime Minister, Lloyd George, seeking and obtaining his support for Scottish home rule. In 1918 the STUC supported the SHRA campaign for separate Scottish representation at the Paris peace talks. In the General Election of that year the Scottish Council of the Labour Party made home rule a major feature of the Labour manifesto, while the Scottish miners became affiliated to the SHRA.

Yet the initial enthusiasm shown by the Labour movement for home rule soon waned, even though there have always been individuals within the movement favourable to the cause. The lessening of Labour enthusiasm led to a questioning within nationalist circles of the advisability of trying to get home rule through the established political parties. The Liberal Party was no longer in serious political contention, and until 1945 the Labour Party was only able to form minority governments or to take part in coalitions. Neither party was in a position to enforce its will against determined opposition, and increasingly within the Labour Party the desire for Scottish autonomy declined. The bloody events in Ireland and the final outcome of devolutionary demands there had not warmed many English hearts to the home-rule cause. Further, in spite of the successful outcome to a war ostensibly fought to defend the rights of small nations, both the left and the right in British politics now saw nationalism as anachronistic. Stanley Baldwin, for example, argued that large units would be more likely to establish world prosperity and that the re-creation of small units would be a retrogressive step. The *Glasgow Herald,* commenting on the election address of the Nationalist candidate in the 1930 East Renfrew by-election, wrote:

The contents cannot be taken seriously by anyone at this critical juncture in the economic life and destiny of the nation. An ego-centric patriotism, such as only the most reactionary type of nationalism produces; convenient blindness to inconvenient facts; and the haziest ideas as to what Scottish self-government would consist in – such things would appear to be the fit trappings for nothing more serious than a crank's hobby horse.

And, as the Labour challenge to the Conservatives increased, the politics of region became for the Labour movement increasingly irrelevant to the real issues – class and the equitable distribution of the social product. The home-rule movement did not appear to provide solutions to problems of poverty and exploitation and would serve to distract attention from these issues and possibly prove divisive as well. From the Marxist point of view the nation-state was merely a phase in social development that would soon pass away when the dominance of the bourgeoisie was smashed. Nationalist disillusion with the Labour movement began as early as 1924 when Ramsay MacDonald, an erstwhile nationalist, proclaimed that while he personally was in favour of some home rule, his Cabinet was not. By 1930 the STUC was seriously considering the possibility of amalgamating with their English counterpart, a suggestion which would have been inconceivable a decade earlier.

But there were more pragmatic reasons for Labour's rejection of the home-rule cause. To Labour strategists of the mid-twenties it seemed that Scotland was to become a Labour stronghold. In 1924, for example, the Labour Party polled 41·1 per cent of the vote in Scotland compared with only 32·9 per cent in England. A legislative assembly in Edinburgh might mean a decrease in the number of Scottish MPs, much as the creation of Stormont had meant a decrease in the number of Ulster representatives. This, it seemed, would lessen Labour's chances of ever being able to form a majority government. At around the same time Labour enthusiasm for proportional representation waned, and for similar reasons. Thus, while in their public stance the Labour Party deferred to the Scottish sense of separate identity, programmatically this manifested itself in administrative rather than legislative devolution. Labour sentiment declined still further when nationalists began to campaign in opposition to them. Although the number of votes nationalist candidates received was usually small, this intervention could be important, especially in by-elections when the electorate is smaller and generally more volatile. When Tom Johnston was defeated by a coalition candidate in 1932 he blamed it on the nationalist intervention.

Conservative support for devolution, which had always been weak, also wavered under increased ideological conflict and the Irish troubles. In 1919 a group of Conservative MPs requested a

Speaker's Conference on devolution. The Conference was chaired by Speaker Lowther, and two reports emerged. Both broadly agreed upon the powers to be devolved, but one recommended an extension of the House of Commons committee system, while the other proposed a federal arrangement. Both reports, though, were agreed that the provincial assembly should have considerable revenue-raising powers.

Tory support for devolution, where it existed, was given generally for two reasons. Firstly, some Conservatives in Scotland felt that Scottish culture was valuable but in danger, and saw a degree of political autonomy as the only way of preserving it against English incursions. In part this was a reaction to the heightened tendency of the state to intervene in more and more areas of life. Secondly, with the growth of government the parliamentary timetable was becoming increasingly congested, and it was believed by a few MPs that the only way to ensure proper legislative scrutiny was to apportion some Government business to regional assemblies. However, this lukewarm Conservative support faded away, and nothing more was heard of either of the schemes proposed by the Speaker's Conference after 1922.

Nationalism between the two World Wars existed only on the fringe of serious politics. It was vociferous, enthusiastic and active. Sometimes the leaders had considerable standing in their own right in other fields, as was the case with Hugh MacDiarmid, Lewis Spence, R. Erskine of Mar and R. B. Cunninghame-Graham. Numerically though, prior to 1932, nationalism as a separate political movement was weak; the vociferous and sometimes spectacular nature of Scottish nationalism after 1928 was to some extent enforced. For the fifty years prior to the First World War the home-rule movement in Scotland may not have achieved its ends, but at least it lived in hope. Scottish home rule, though far from becoming a burning parliamentary question, did have a fairly regular body of support, and the home-rule issue was articulated with some success within the political system. Nationalism became a separate political interest in Scotland only after it had been rejected by the two most powerful established parties. The National Party of Scotland was formed in 1928 by the fusion of a number of small nationalist groups with the express intention of reinstating home rule as an issue on the political agenda. Since the nationalist interest had been excluded by the major established parties, the only entrée was through the ballot-box in competition with those parties.

Rejected as irrelevant to contemporary British problems, anachronistic, divisive, and a potential instigator of violence, the NPS had a considerable public relations job to do before recognition could be expected. There were some in the NPS who expected instant support, while others realized that success would only come when the conditions were right. In general the Press were not on the side of the nationalists, although in a fight for circulation in 1932 the *Scottish Daily Express* and the *Daily Record* accorded them extra publicity. The *Scottish Daily Express* actually ran a straw poll in 35,000 homes and found 113,000 people in favour of self-government with less than 5,000 opposed. Usually, though, the Press noticed the nationalists in their frequent moments of dissension heightening the public image of a squabbling, unsettled party.

The dissension within the NPS and later the Scottish National Party arose from two causes. Firstly the leadership, especially of the NPS, was not particularly suited to running a successful, democratic political party. The leadership group included a large core of intellectuals and firebrands, and such people are not easily persuaded to act in concert. The skill of the intellectual is his ability to categorize, rearrange and manipulate concepts into a coherent and often persuasive format. A political party needs such persons for they provide a creative element. But the dominance of intellectuals usually means that there is no 'party line', the love of debate and dispute taking precedence over the need to present a unified front. Principle is seen as being more important than practice. Further, such people are often temperamentally unsuited to the routine necessary in building or maintaining a political party. The lack of any real prospect of attaining an appreciable degree of power meant that there were even fewer constraints upon behaviour. Dissension in the nationalist camp did not appear to have much cost. An element of stability was provided by Muirhead, a meticulous bureaucrat, and John M. MacCormick who was very much a political pragmatist.

Secondly, though, there were genuine policy disputes within both the NPS and the SNP. These disputes had to be resolved before there was any possibility of popular nationalist success, and between 1928 and 1956 each of the major issues that divided nationalists was resolved. Usually the settlement occurred not through concurrence but through defection, the dissident elements periodically sloughing off from the main stem of nationalism and attempting to achieve their ends elsewhere, leaving the SNP in an ideologically more unified state. It is quite possible that the SNP after 1962 would have gained some electoral success whatever the state of the party, but it is unlikely that it would have maintained that progress had all the issues that split it in the 1930s remained unsettled. Not even the prospect of power could have held such a party together for fourteen years.

There were four major areas of disagreement within the party at this time. Firstly, there was the question of how much devolution was sought. Secondly, there was debate as to whether the pre-independence party had the right to put forward policies that an independent Scottish Parliament might not accept. Thirdly, there was a continual, if at times low-key, struggle between the left and right within the party. Lastly, there was controversy as to the best means of attaining nationalist ends.

It would be incorrect to consider the movement factionalized in the decade following 1928. It was not always possible to predict an individual's position on a range of issues if only one issue position was known; different coalitions would form around the issue being debated. Further, on many issues there were not clear alternatives; often there were many positions each with a body of adherents. But, while the NPS, and later the SNP, did not split into formal factions, the different issues were not unrelated.

Four basic positions can be discerned on the independence issue. Firstly, there were the devolutionists who, in the main, desired a weak form of federalism with Westminster remaining supreme. Among those supporting the devolutionist position were those who favoured a 'stepping-stones' approach, and sought to bring about increased Scottish autonomy through small, piecemeal gains. These adherents came mostly from the Scottish Party which amalgamated with the NPS in 1934 to form the SNP. The 'federalist' position was held by those who wanted considerable autonomy for Scotland, yet felt that complete separation was impracticable. A proviso of this position was that the extent of cooperation would have to await the decision of a Scottish Parliament. These two positions were held both as a matter of principle and also as a matter of practical politics; it was considered impracticable to campaign for more than would be acceptable to the Scottish public and more than could be given by the Westminster Government. There were two separatist positions: that which aimed for complete separation and that which sought dominion status for Scotland. To achieve dominion recognition for Scotland the SNP lobbied the Imperial Conference in 1930, as well as setting up a provisional government. Duncan H. McNeill, 'foreign secretary' in the provisional government, recalls that the only favourable responses to his overtures were from some of the Canadian provinces. But there was even division within the dominion school, between those who, because Scotland was instrumental in founding the Empire, believed that her Parliament should be accorded Mother Parliament status equal with Westminster, and those who would accept a status equal to that of Canada or Australia. Such debates, though, in the political climate of the times were rather academic.

The question as to whether the SNP should campaign on a comprehensive platform arose through the desire of the leadership group to avoid bringing the potential divisions within the party into the open. The NPS put forward the view that they could not usurp the right of a future Scottish parliament by deciding policies that would prejudice the actions of that parliament. As a letter in *Forward* in 1933 explained, the question of autonomy was the only matter in which the NPS could claim competence:

> With regard to other questions, the views of the individual members differ widely; but all agree that, whatever their views on any question affecting Scotland, they will accept the decision of the future Scottish National Parliament, whether they approve of it or not.

Theoretically, this was a splendid way of avoiding divisive issues within the NPS and limiting debate to the best way of achieving independence. Until 1933 there was an attempt to shelve responsibility onto the future assembly. The problem was, as Arthur Donaldson forcefully pointed out, the electorate was unlikely to vote for the NPS unless they were aware at least in broad outline what a future independent Scotland would look like and how it would differ from the contemporary one. The NPS was asking the electorate to sign a blank cheque. There were resignations from the NPS when it did not put forward policies, and resignations when it did, but in the long term the problem was solved for the SNP by the secession of almost half the party in 1942.

The problems raised by the statement of policy aims lessened for the SNP with the passage of time, due largely to fortuitous circumstances. Between 1932 and 1937 the NPS and the SNP were relieved of many of the extremists on both political wings. After the First World War there was a great deal of support for the home-rule cause in radical circles. The Labour Party, however, attempted to dissuade its members from joining the SHRA, in many cases unsuccessfully, so that, when the SHRA fused with other nationalist associations to form the NPS, many of the members of the new party were also members of the Labour Party. The same applied to the other two established parties, though to a lesser degree. When the NPS began to campaign electorally, they did not insist that their members resign from other parties. Instead, a number of verbal solutions were proposed to wallpaper over the problem, often instigated by John MacCormick. In 1928 the NPS decided that members should not 'normally' support candidates other than those put up by the party; the NPS put up so few candidates that a conflict of loyalties was comparatively rare. But in 1935 a resolution was put to the Annual Conference to the effect that no member of the SNP could also be a member of an 'English-controlled party'. This was defeated, but an amendment carried to the effect that no office-bearer in the SNP could take part in the work of an English-controlled party. As with the rejection of a comprehensive social policy, the leadership was walking a delicate path designed to avoid bringing the radical-conservative split into the open.

Events aided them in their task. The merger of the Scottish Party and the NPS in 1934 led to widescale defections by radicals in the branches. The Scottish Party was a breakaway section of the Cathcart Conservative Association and among its leaders were such high-status persons as the Duke of Montrose and Sir Alexander McEwan. The introduction into the nationalist movement of this right-wing element was not to the liking of many socialist members, whose sensitivities were not soothed when Montrose used the nationalist Press to inveigh against hikers disturbing his grouse moors. The merger was largely the work of John MacCormick. His reasons were that the NPS was in very ill straits financially, needed high-status, 'respectable' leaders, and that the two nationalist parties would not be competing against one another. The cost of the merger, apart from the defections, was a modification of the NPS constitution to a slightly less extreme form. By 1936 most of those who had come to the SNP with the Scottish Party had left, dismayed by the socialist tendencies of the party. The constitution was duly re-amended back to its original form. So in a few short years the nationalist party had shed both its extreme wings, allowing the emergence of a policy that was not dominated entirely by either. Left and right still existed within the SNP, as they do today, but no longer threatened to tear the party apart.

The most difficult issue that the nationalist movement had to resolve, and which caused more problems than any other, was the question as to the best means of achieving nationalist influence at Westminster. After the exclusion of the nationalist interest from politics, the NPS was formed to contest elections and force concessions from the major parties. The all-party approach and its variant, the attempt to work through one-party, had failed, and the conventional electoral strategy seemed the only alternative. The immediate cause of the formation ofthe NPS was the rejection of a home-rule bill in Parliament following two years of campaigning, but unfortunately electoral campaigning seemed to achieve little either. Generally nationalist candidates lost their deposits, the party spent money it could ill afford, in spite of the generosity of R. E. Muirhead, and got very little in the way of results.

Opinions within both the NPS and the SNP were very divided. One view was that the attempt to contest elections should be deferred until a coherent social policy had been formulated. Another view maintained that elections were too expensive and that the money was better spent in other ways: arranging plebiscites, putting pressure on candidates of other parties, and on publicity, in an attempt to rouse Scottish public opinion to such a pitch as to enforce a response from other parties. Yet another view argued that rather than the electoral approach aiding the nationalist cause, it was actively hindering it by rousing the opposition of the other parties. Rather than leading to a favourable consensus among the other parties, by becoming electoral competitors the NPS had forced the opposite consensus, so that the two major parties were now united in their rejection of home rule. This group advocated a return to the old all-party approach and received encouragement from the other parties, especially Labour and Liberal.

In fact, the very act of the nationalists entering the electoral arena had changed the logic of the situation. Prior to this the home-rule issue could be viewed by the major parties as a possible means of getting votes. The nationalists could pose a threat to the parties that could not be properly evaluated. In such a situation the party managers saw that it was an interest that at least ought to be deferred to if not actually accommodated. Having campaigned and failed badly, though, the nationalists exposed the inability of the home-rule cause to mobilize the electorate, and thus allowed the major parties to take even less notice of it.

Given this situation, the attempt to influence the major parties through either the all-party, single-party, or propaganda approach was doomed to failure because there was no pressure that the nationalists could bring to bear and no sanctions that they could apply. MacCormick did not recognize this until the very end of his career, although others within the SNP did, and continued to urge an electoral approach as the only way forward. In this opinion the only alternative to the ballot-box was the gun or the bomb. A member of the National Council, indeed, wrote in a private letter:

> But revolutions are rarely gentlemanly affairs ... since the war Ireland, India, Egypt and Palestine have taught the lesson – can Scotland expect to escape the same necessity?

This was very much a minority opinion. Scotland was not Ireland. Violence would, as nationalists had long recognized, do their cause far more harm than good. Within nationalist ranks, indeed, there was a strong element of pacifism, the moral rejection of violence as a means to achieve political ends. R. E. Muirhead personified this element and in his frustrated search for a more militant nationalism finally turned to passive resistance.

Although the exclusion from orthodox politics was the occasion for the formation of a separate nationalist party, there were other conditions that militated towards this end. In very many ways the First World War was a watershed in British life: it was the first 'total' war, in the sense that it involved all sections of British society and the Government increasingly intervened in society as a whole. There was a massive move towards centralized direction that was not reversed when the war ended. Further, after the war the progress that had hitherto marked the Scottish economy was not maintained.

In 1906 the wages paid in many Scottish industries were considerably higher than those paid in England; shipbuilding, carpets, baking and confectionery, building, grain-milling and the boot and shoe industry are all examples of this, and the money earned by women was higher in nearly all industries. In 1900 the taxable receipts for Scotland as a percentage of the United Kingdom total was 11·9 per cent, a figure considerably in excess of the proportion of the United Kingdom population that was Scottish. By 1929 this figure had dropped to 7·9 per cent. The Great Depression brought further troubles to Scotland: in 1932 nearly 28 per cent of the labour force was unemployed, and in 1938 it was still as high as 16 per cent.

In such a situation it is not surprising that a militant nationalist movement should arise, but most of the discontent was mobilized by the Labour Party, while the NPS and the SNP stood on the fringes. It was not apparent to most people that nationalism had any ready solution for the troubles that beset Scotland, while the Labour Party had a coherent policy and promised to aid those most disadvantaged in society. Many of the early nationalists, although perturbed by the economic state of Scotland, were in the main motivated by a fear for Scottish culture which they saw as being increasingly anglicized. But the survival of a Scottish dialect means little to an unemployed factory worker when others are promising more work or unemployment benefits. It is noticeable that since its early days as a political party the cultural content of the SNP programme has become less obvious, and the emphasis upon economic and social matters greater. The nationalist political party, which began by stressing on every occasion the unique cultural identity of the Scottish people, now assumes it. No longer does it need to be stressed, but merely mobilized from time to time.

The importance of the period between the two World Wars lay in the fact that in this period the major problems confronting a nationalist movement were raised and various solutions canvassed. The movement was to be torn apart on two further occasions before internal agreement was reached; the initial step, though, had been taken.

CHAPTER FIVE

The Development of the SNP

The Scottish National Party was, as we have seen, divided on a number of issues, with genuine differences of view being overlaid by personality differences. The disputes within the SNP were disabling, but the fragmented nature of the movement was made worse by the small groups outside the Party pursuing similar ends by different means. The SNP's lack of success meant that it was unable to exert any control over the schismatic groups in spite of its numerical predominance. To add to its difficulties, the SNP was in financial difficulties just prior to the Second World War: in July 1939 the Party had an overdraft of over £800 and a membership very much lower than that of 1932. It was the financial consideration that prevented the Party from contesting the 1938 Bridgeton by-election, causing Wendy Wood to resign and stand as an independent.

The disarray with which the nationalist movement faced the Scottish voter until after 1955 did not pass without comment from within and outwith the Movement. Roland Muirhead despairingly wrote in 1950 that 'the longer I live the more I feel that the lack of ability to cooperate is the weakest spot of us Scots'. This was shortly after Muirhead, a founder member of the NPS, had organized the Scottish National Congress. An office bearer in the Congress was W. Oliver Brown who wrote in his *Witdom*, with humour and perhaps just a grain of truth, that 'I bitterly regret the day when I compromised the unity of my party by admitting a second member'. More seriously the *Observer* (2/8/54) commented that 'the nationalist movement is all individuals and fragments, a collection of oddities and hopefuls with a bewildering history of schism'.

The 'fundamentalists' and the home-rulers after 1939 came more and more into conflict within the SNP. The period between 1939 and 1950 can be seen as a time when the two sides separated out, each to go its own way. Increasingly the fundamentalists won control, and the home-rulers had to seek a means of expression outside the SNP. However, the moderates won a small victory in 1939 and 1940, when it was resolved that membership of both the United Scotsmen and SNP was not possible. The United Scotsmen was an organization that attempted to unite militant nationalists, and it was outlawed by the SNP. They were primarily a propagandist group, and they disagreed with MacCormick's flirtation with other political parties. But while their exclusion reduced the number of militants within the SNP, after the 1942 split and the secession of the moderate faction many of them rejoined the SNP.

These events of 1939–40 were stimulated by the movement of the SNP – mainly under the guidance of John MacCormick – back towards the old all-party approach which had been rejected in 1928 when the NPS was formed. The reason for the formation of the NPS had been the failure by various nationalist bodies, but especially the second SHRA, to persuade the major parties to grant some legislative authority to Scotland. The two SHRAs had tried this approach for fifty years, before the nationalist interest was finally denied meaningful parliamentary expression. But, after ten years of unhappy experience at the polls, the SNP was preparing to do an about-turn. Having, though, demonstrated the inability of nationalism to mobilize a significant Scottish vote, the nationalist negotiating position was very much weaker than it had been prior to 1928.

The move back towards an all-party approach, while doubtless stimulated by electoral failure, was also partly in response to greater interest in devolution within the Labour Party. In 1939 a great many of the administrative functions of the Scottish Office were moved to Edinburgh from London. In 1938 a circular issued by the Labour Council for Scottish Self-Government stated that:

We feel that the cause of self-government is one which must be brought to the attention of every true Scot, especially that on Socialist lines.

MacCormick was also in touch with the London Scots Self-Government Committee, a radical Labour organization, with some of the Scots Labour MPs as members. Its president was Thomas Johnston, the War-time Secretary of State for Scotland. At this time it was still possible to be a member of the SNP and a member of another political party, which created to some extent a bridge between the SNP and the Labour and Liberal Parties. Further, in 1937–8 there were negotiations with the Liberals over establishing an electoral pact whereby the Liberals and the Nationalists would support one another and not compete in some constituencies. The favourable sentiments towards devolution expressed in the 1942 Scottish Estimates debate in Parliament also seemed to suggest that the all-party approach might work.

On the very eve of war it seemed as if the moderate faction had won. In May 1939 a national plebiscite was arranged, though never put into effect. Also in 1939 a National Convention was to be held in Glasgow with representatives from the parties, burghs and corporations. It was especially hoped that through the Convention the Communist Party could be drawn into home-rule activity. This kind of programme was very much a return to the all-party approach and disliked by the fundamentalists. As it was, the National Convention was abandoned due to the outbreak of war.

The division between the home-rulers and the fundamentalists over the right degree of devolution and the best approach to its attainment was basic. For the purposes of practical politics, though, they may have coexisted in reasonable harmony – in much the same way as the Manifesto and Tribune factions of the Labour Party do today – had it not been for the fact that this basic cleavage in the SNP was reinforced by a split regarding proper nationalist attitudes to the war. The question was whether, and to what degree, the nationalists should support the war effort. The Party had always included a number of pacifists for whom war of any kind was to be opposed and it also had a number of republicans for whom the appeal of king and country was slight. More importantly, however, it was argued that a British Government did not have the right to commit Scotland to a war without the consent of the Scottish people. The Scottish parliamentary representatives were not considered competent to give such a commitment.

Tactically the SNP was in a somewhat difficult position and the situation of the leaders was wholly unenviable. Many SNP members had as much dislike of Fascism and its activities as the most chauvinistic Englishman. On the other hand they had spent the last dozen years denying the right of the British Government to legislate on behalf of Scotland. Within the SNP the hard-liners took the view that, insofar as was possible, the SNP should not cooperate with the government especially with regard to conscription. The moderates, on the other hand, recognized that the majority of Scots supported the British Government wholeheartedly, and that to push an anti-war line could alienate a large section of the Scottish public who were, if not supporters of the SNP, at least sympathetic to the movement. Indeed, many of the pro-war faction were genuine in their support. The Covenant Association, where many of the moderates later went, was very loyal to the Crown and to the idea of the United Kingdom. Also, since the moderate faction was negotiating with both the Labour and Liberal Parties, a charge of disloyalty could have severely weakened their negotiating position. The war issue was important within the SNP between 1937 and 1942. Strangely, while the fundamentalists, who included in the main the hard-liners on the war issue, won control of the Party in 1942, their views about the war were either not picked up by the public or were ignored. The SNP got extremely good election results in by-elections in 1943, 1944 and 1945, the first of these being contested by Douglas Young who was prosecuted for refusing to be conscripted. However, by 1943 it was probably difficult for the Scottish public to know exactly where the SNP stood on the war issue, such was the confusion within the movement.

As early as July 1934 there was a nationalist Anti-Conscription League with 'Membership open to all who hold that the violation of the Treaty of Union (1707) exempts Scotland and Scottish citizens from conscription and military service of any description under British powers'. The hard-liners within the SNP won the day at the 1937 Annual Conference when a resolution was passed – a weaker version of a more militant resolution – that concluded:

... all male members of the Scottish National Party of military age hereby pledge themselves to refuse to serve with any section of the Crown forces until the programme of the Scottish National Party has been fulfilled.

This position had moderated somewhat by 1939 when in the October manifesto the SNP declared that Scotland would fight with England and the Commonwealth for ideals appealing to the Scottish people.

A hypothetical war in the future, the phoney war, and then the real thing, however, were very different, and the last produced a further modification of the SNP position although the Scottish Neutrality League, composed of hard-line nationalists, maintained the militant position outside the SNP. With regard to rearmament a SNL official wrote in 1939 that 'in their desire to retain world domination, England's rulers have gone crazy at our expense' and 'England will fight to the last Scot'. Even after the war the case was made that Scots had suffered a disproportionate number of casualties during the war, which echoed similar allegations made after the First World War.

On 16 December 1939 the SNP held a special conference to decide their collective attitude to the war. In their pamphlet *Peace and War* they agreed to support the Government in a war against a country that had destroyed three nations. They did, however, send a letter to Secretary of State Colville urging the Government to state its war aims. When the minister did not reply, the SNP amended its support, and attempted to protect those of its members who maintained the hard line. The Resolution read:

This Party, while recognizing that the majority of the Scottish people have acquiesced in conscription as a necessity in the present emergency, nevertheless consider and will strongly urge that the definition of conscientious objection should be enlarged to include objections based on profound political conviction.

The exact position of the SNP regarding the war was so unclear by this time that it is hardly surprising that their war aims had no electoral impact. With the ball passing rapidly between the hard-liners and the moderates, with the pragmatic MacCormick searching for a verbal formula that would keep the Party together, the SNP position on the war before 1942 was extremely unstable. In Scotland's Charter of Freedoms, a ten-point summary of the aims of the SNP which was adopted at the Annual Conference of 1940, there is no mention of the war at all. The *Scots Independent,* under the editorship of John Mac-Donald, however, was urging Churchill to fortify the Cheviots with a view to making a stand in Scotland should the South of England be invaded.

From a British point of view it was probably of no importance where the SNP stood on the war issue. The Party had shrunk considerably since its heyday in 1932–4, and it had very little influence. Clearly though, both the German propaganda machine and the British Government thought them important. The Germans opened a radio station – Radio Caledonia – in an attempt to spread disaffection with the Union, while the Government arrested a number of nationalists including the pacifist R. E. Muirhead. Col. M. Muriel Gibson, the present National Secretary of the SNP, maintains she was kept under surveillance for several months after helping Arthur Donaldson with his office work.

From the point of view of the SNP and the development of nationalism, the war question was of vital importance. The war issue acted as a catalyst making the various factions coalesce into two main camps which then split the Party. It can be argued that before 1937, although there were policy and personality differences within the Party, the same people were not always on the same side on every issue. Thus, although there were acrimonious debates on all the important issues, the

Party was not factionalized. This is very much the case with the present Party. However, after 1937 two distinct factions began to emerge, and the hard-liners on the war issue tended to be fundamentalists with regard to the amount of devolution desired; they also tended to favour an electoral strategy. The contradictory nature of the SNP approach to the war was largely due to the competition between these factions. The reality was, needless to say, a little more complex than this. For example, Douglas Young who took over the Chairmanship of the Party in 1942, was a hard-liner on the war issue but a moderate with regard to other issues. Also, some of those who followed Young on the war issue were to leave the Party in 1946 on the issue of exclusive party membership and the electoral policy of the SNP. Like most social generalizations it holds only approximately. However, even if the question of the nationalist attitude to the war had not been the immediate cause, it is probable that sooner or later such a split would have occurred.

The break-up of the SNP occurred at the Annual Conference of 1942. William Power, the council nominee for the Chairmanship of the Party was narrowly defeated by Douglas Young, who claimed the right to be a conscientious objector on political grounds and was sentenced to a year's imprisonment for his beliefs. The meeting was noisy and acrimonious, and even today some bitterness remains. It was alleged then, and has been repeated many times since, that the coup against the MacCormick faction was engineered by the creation of fictitious branches which then sent delegates to swell the vote against MacCormick. Whether this is true or not is irrelevant historically; the immediate issue merely precipitated what was in any case likely to happen.

The split in 1942 had a decisive effect on the future of Scottish nationalism. MacCormick, following the defeat of his candidate, seceded from the SNP, followed by large numbers of delegates. They immediately set up the Scottish Union, which soon became the Scottish Convention, which eventually became the Scottish Covenant Association. The Convention and the Covenant Association had a powerful initial impact, and may be seen in the role of John the Baptist to the later advent of the SNP as a potent electoral force. The inspired publicity and propaganda methods initiated by MacCormick may well have had some effect in preparing Scottish public opinion. At the same time the existence of a successful nationalist organization outside the SNP considerably simplified the policy options open to the SNP. The fertile moderate ground had been captured, leaving the SNP to till the stony extremist ground. Further, after 1945 the spotlight was taken off the SNP, leaving them, after the further secession of 1946, in relative peace to develop policies with a small and reasonably unified Party. The failure of the Covenant Association strengthened the SNP argument that power would only come through electoral success. This debate, though, was not finally resolved until the mid-1950s – R. E. Muirhead left the SNP on this issue; in reality the failure of the propagandist all-party approach left no alternative open to the nationalists other than to contest national elections.

Between 1928 and 1955 nationalist fortunes revolved to a large extent around the figure of John MacCormick. While R. E. Muirhead was an equally ubiquitous activist, his formality and reticence did not make him a natural leader. Rather, he exerted influence through the constancy of his endeavour, his high work-rate and dedication to the cause, and his capacity to finance various nationalist activities. MacCormick was a more flamboyant figure, and by all accounts a brilliant orator. While still a student at Glasgow University he was a key figure in the amalgamation of organizations that led to the formation of the NPS. It was he who was the prime mover in the merger with the Scottish Party in 1934, which led to the resignation from the SNP of so many nationalists. It was MacCormick who incurred the displeasure of both the fundamentalists and the Party right wing by his flirtation with the Liberals and Labour. And, in 1942, he was a central figure in the SNP split, after which he had the most outstanding nationalist organization that Scotland to that date had seen.

What manner of man was John MacCormick? In politics

he must be considered a pragmatist. Had he paused amid his vast activity to discuss the nature of politics, he too would probably have called it 'the art of the possible'. Thus, while he was far from averse to the grand gesture, never being a man to eschew publicity, he was not temperamentally drawn to utopian positions. Thus the attempt to achieve total independence for Scotland was abandoned early in his career, and he concentrated upon what he considered attainable, using whatever tools were at hand at any particular time. He was consistent only to the end of increased autonomy for Scotland, and was inconsistent in his choice of means to achieve this end. Seen in this light many of the apparent contradictions in his career disappear. In 1928, when the nationalist interest appeared to have been rejected at Westminster, electoral confrontation appeared the only way forward. In 1934 he was prepared to decimate the Party in order to achieve unity with the Scottish Party, in order to present a united nationalist electoral front, to bolster the sagging finances of the NPS, and to utilize electorally the high-status leaders of the Scottish Party. By 1938 he had had second thoughts about electoral strategy and began manoeuvring to get accepted as Party policy that which he had explicitly rejected in 1928. MacCormick's pragmatism was anathema to many nationalists. His popularity was not improved by his authoritarian running of the SNP. As Dr MacDonald put it, 'He was unwilling to accept any idea that was not his own'. But, with Muirhead, he helped the SNP through some of its most difficult years, for by 1939 the membership had shrunk to less than two thousand from ten thousand in 1934. Some of the shrinkage, though, might be attributed to his own activities.

Unfortunately for MacCormick, his highly developed tactical sense was not matched by a strategic awareness. All his efforts through a propagandist all-party approach were unvailing, given the logic of the situation. Without votes in a parliamentary election, Government was not going to recognize nationalism as a political force. Concessions were made administratively, largely due to pressures from within Parliament, but any progress towards a legislative devolution would have to

await the proof that a demand existed, and the only acceptable
evidence was votes. The nationalists having failed at the polls
could not expect their demands to be met, for it could be
argued that they were not truly representative of Scottish
opinion. But this was also true of the all-party propagandist
approach. The SNP, if the vote is taken as the only adequate
criterion, had proved that demand did not exist. Governments in
liberal-democracies respond to pressure, and there appeared to
be little pressure for legislative devolution. Had MacCormick
understood the situation fully then doubtless he would have
tempered his pragmatism.

Thus, while the Scottish Convention and the Covenant Association were splendid failures, they were always doomed to
fail. The most they achieved was a Royal Commission and a
committee to inquire into the collection of Scottish financial
statistics. MacCormick's approach could succeed in the present-
day situation, when it has been shown that nationalism pos-
sesses electoral appeal, but then of course the propagandist approach is unnecessary.

After MacCormick and his followers had seceded from the
SNP and set up the Scottish Union and then the Scottish Convention, the SNP began to achieve some electoral success. In
1943 and 1944 they got substantial by-election results, and in
1945 actually won Motherwell, although losing it a few months
later at the General Election. The party truce that was observed
by the major parties throughout the war did not affect the SNP,
and they were able to mobilize the anti-Government vote. The
Party's success was due rather to peculiar circumstances than to
any particular virtue attributed to the SNP by the Scottish
public. Yet it is interesting to note that it was apparently
psychologically easy for the Scottish voter to switch to an SNP
vote when other political pressures were not present. As we
shall see, one factor in the emergence of the SNP as a political
power in the 1960s was the decline in partisanship and major
party loyalty, which retrospectively we can see presaged by the
SNP by-election successes during the war years. At the 1945
General Election the nationalist vote collapsed entirely and

thereafter the Party was eclipsed by the Convention and the Covenant. Roland Muirhead criticized the SNP after 1945 for 'bleating' about what the Government should be doing rather than spending 'more of its energy in ways and means of worrying the Government', while Arthur Donaldson had written a little earlier that 'the SNP is not dying, it is merely mummifying'. In fact, in terms of policy construction the SNP was quite active up to 1946, but the cost of political purity after the 1942 and 1946 secessions was a certain loss of dynamism. The SNP to some extent then withdrew into a shell, and it was the Convention that represented Scottish nationalism in the public mind.

In the 1945 General Election the Scottish Convention circularized all the parliamentary candidates to ascertain their views on self-government. The idea was to swing public opinion and votes behind those candidates who were most nationalistic, and to persuade the candidates of the value of a public commitment to home rule. The latter aim was certainly achieved. It was not unusual for all the candidates in a constituency to profess national sentiments although, of course, this meant different things to different people. The candidates' nationalistic fervour was doubtless enhanced by Dr Robert McIntyre's success for the SNP at Motherwell. Hector McNeil, a later Secretary of State for Scotland, in a competitively nationalist frame of mind at the hustings, required nothing less than complete public exposure on this point:

If my Tory opponent is unwilling to pledge himself to a measure of self-government, he should take off the kilt he wears and not attempt to mislead the people into thinking him a patriotic Scot.

However, all the questionnaires sent out by the Convention produced only 126 responses from the candidates, of which only six were definitely against some measure of home rule. The Labour Party manifesto for the 1945 General Election did not, in fact, mention devolution; social reform was the dominant theme. The Scottish Council of the Labour Party, though, put out a Scottish manifesto in which 'A Scottish Parliament for

Scottish affairs' came as second priority after a commitment to the defeat of Japan.

In 1947 the Scottish Convention called a Scottish National Assembly, which was chaired by John MacCormick who went out of his way to stress that the Assembly was not a creature of the Convention but a genuine national gathering. In the Report of Proceedings the Assembly was described as a 'landmark in Scottish history' and claimed to be:

... more widely representative than the momentous Glasgow General Assembly of 1638, or even the old Scottish Parliament. It was, in fact, the largest and most widely representative meeting ever held in Scotland to discuss the most centrally vital of Scottish matters, namely, the government of Scotland.

About four hundred people attended, including representatives from all the political parties, the Church, cultural organizations, trade unions, large and small burghs, and business. The Assembly debated three resolutions, and eventually accepted one of them by a massive majority, rejecting a milder version. The accepted resolution read, in part:

This Assembly, representative of all shades of opinion in Scotland, is convinced that a substantial majority of the Scottish people favours a large measure of self-government, and therefore resolves to request that the Government should forthwith introduce in Parliament a Bill to give effect to the Scottish Self-Government proposals ...

The resolution was probably correct in its view that a large number of Scots favoured some measure of self-government. The *Scottish Daily Express* and *Daily Record* polls of 1932 and the Kirriemuir Plebiscite of 1949 – which registered over ninety-two per cent as being in favour – as well as the massive enthusiasm that greeted the Scottish Covenant, all seem to attest to this fact. Neither were the major party politicians unaware of the desire, for while being unwilling to act to secure legislative devolution, they would frequently defer verbally to this public want on the campaign platform. Nor were the nationalists unaware of the sympathy their cause aroused. As far back as 1929

Iain Gilles had written on the occasion of Muirhead's lost deposit in the West Renfrewshire by-election:

> We shall for five, ten maybe fifteen years – until British party politics are thoroughly discredited – receive infinitely more sympathy than votes.

The paradox of Scottish nationalism, of which the early nationalists were aware and which must have been very frustrating for them, was that at any one point in time the majority of Scots did want more self-government, although not independence, but that it seemed impossible to translate this desire into votes. Tom Johnston during the war made his cabinet colleagues uncomfortably aware of this widespread but latent sentiment, and used the spectre of a resurgent political nationalism to obtain economic and administrative concessions for Scotland. But, even now, when nationalism is clearly such a powerful political force, in the results of surveys into public attitudes in Scotland devolution comes very low down the list. Education, inflation, housing and old age pensions are all considered more important. But if the public are specifically asked about the devolution, then a majority will reply that Scotland needs more self-government. The problem facing the nationalists is to increase the salience of nationalism to the individual, and the intensity with which he experiences it. It has to be shown that a sense of Scottishness is a politically relevant factor. Within the voter's political world-view his sense of Scottish identity had to be moved from a politically peripheral position to a central position. And, once that had occurred in a sufficiently large number of cases, then the dimensions of political debate would have been changed. The politics of region would then have replaced the politics of class.

The 1947 Scottish National Assembly approved a committee to consider the details of a self-government bill. The committee reported back to the second Scottish National Assembly in March 1948. They advocated a Scottish Parliament with substantial internal autonomy, central government retaining control over such things as defence, foreign affairs, and the coinage.

The financial arrangements recommended, which later became part of the Scottish Convention programme, were that, while indirect taxation should be levied by central government in order to avoid a customs barrier between Scotland and England, direct taxation should be controlled by the Scottish Parliament.

The Assembly proposals made no headway in Parliament whatsoever, although launched in a blaze of optimism. There were several reasons for this. Even had the Labour Government evinced any great interest it is unlikely that time could have been found in a very crowded parliamentary timetable for a home-rule bill. Neither is it at all certain that a majority existed in Parliament for such a bill. Further, while the Assembly was prestigious in terms of those attending it, it carried little political weight. Its lack of continuity meant it could apply no consistent pressure, while to achieve this, given the geographical and political diversity of its membership, would have required a degree of coordination that just was not available. At best the Assembly was a good public relations exercise for the nationalist movement.

The following year, 1949, the Scottish Convention presented the Scottish Covenant to the public. The idea was not new; MacCormick had suggested something similar in 1935, but the method of its implementation was strikingly original. A constant finding in social psychology is that active participation in a project leaves a very much stronger impression on the individual than does passive acceptance or agreement. The Covenant was surrounded with a vast amount of publicity, and at the same time required at least some personal commitment, in that it required a signature. The wording of the Covenant was as follows:

We, the people of Scotland who subscribe this engagement, declare our belief that reform in the constitution of our country is necessary to secure good government in accordance with our Scottish traditions and to promote the spiritual and economic welfare of our nation.

We affirm that the desire for such reform is both deep and widespread through the whole community, transcending all political differences and sectional interests, and we undertake to continue in purpose for its achievement.

With that end in view we solemnly enter into the Covenant whereby we pledge ourselves, in all loyalty to the Crown, and within the framework of the United Kingdom, to do everything in our power to secure for Scotland a Parliament with adequate legislative authority in Scottish affairs.

The strength of this document was that emotionally it could unite disparate groups with varying social aims. Its weakness was that it did not commit anyone to any specific action. It managed to unite only by being vague. Had it been presented today, Liberal, Conservative and Labour supporters could all sign it with a clear conscience, for the terms of the Covenant would be interpreted in the light of all three, quite different, devolution positions.

However, within a week of its launching, the Covenant had been signed by 50,000 people, and within two years two to two and a half million signatures had been appended. The exact number, understandably, is uncertain, but should anyone require greater precision the lists still exist. In fact, the figure is probably somewhat inflated, but the response was still impressive.

With the success of the Covenant, the Scottish Convention metamorphosed into the Scottish Covenant Association. The Association attempted to present the signatures to the Prime Minister, and then the Leader of the Opposition, but neither would receive the Association representatives, Churchill's feelings on federation apparently having changed since his days as MP for Dundee. Instead, the representatives met Hector McNeil, the Secretary of State for Scotland, as well as the Conservative spokesmen James Stuart and Walter Elliot. The Conservatives promised a Royal Commission, while Labour set up the Catto Committee to examine the collection of financial statistics for Scotland. The *Highlands and Islands Covenanter* of November 1952 wrote of the Catto Committee, with some justification: 'It met, it reported, it made no-one very much the wiser.' The Balfour Commission report did not favour the nationalist cause either, recommending in the main no constitutional changes.

Following the secession in 1942, the SNP made some initial progress under the Secretaryship of Dr Robert McIntyre, who became the Party's first MP in 1945. An increase in the number of branches and a sixty per cent increase in membership was reported in 1943. The financial position of the Party improved momentarily, although in 1946 Arthur Donaldson wrote '. . . it has not been easy this last twelve-months to keep our heads above water', and by 1947 the Party was having difficulty in meeting its liabilities. A further secession from the SNP occurred in 1946; this time the question of contesting elections was reinforced by the Party deciding to forbid dual political membership. The moderates lost on both issues and a large number of members resigned from the Party. The electoral issue arose again in 1946 due to the collapse of the SNP vote in the 1945 General Election, and given the financial position of the Party it was suggested that the money might be more productively spent in other ways. The 1946 decision did not close the question, however, for periodically it was raised again throughout the 1950s. The old campaigner Roland Muirhead – a survivor from the first SHRA and a founder member of the NPS – eventually left the SNP over this issue. He had earlier set up the Scottish National Congress as an SNP ginger group, and after his resignation the Congress pursued a totally separate policy. Muirhead at this stage of his long career drew his inspiration from India's Congress Party, and believed that the Scottish National Congress should set up a provisional Government. A provisional Government had, of course, been set up in 1931. Muirhead was a pacifist and wholly against the use of violence, but at the age of ninety-one was still an active and militant nationalist. He could see, though, no way the nationalists could achieve their ends through the normal political process. He now concluded that:

Congress believes that there is no hope of getting power by normal parliamentary means. We advocate non-cooperation on the lines of Gandhi.

One of his followers, to her credit, actually refused to pay her wireless licence fee, though also taking the precaution of getting rid of the wireless in good time. But, as with so many nationalist organizations prior to the 1960s, dissension seemed to be a built-in factor. Oliver Brown resigned due to the inefficiency of the organization. Following the 1958 Annual General Meeting Roland Muirhead wrote:

It is saddening to have experienced such happenings ... The exhibition of human depravity was quite beyond anything which I had experienced at any of the Scottish nationalist meetings which I have yet attended.

By 1960 Congress was a spent force. It had never carried any great weight but by 1959 many of its branches, including those at Aberdeen and Edinburgh, had become inactive. The Scottish National Congress was the Grand Old Man's last major effort, although in 1960 he formed a new newspaper (*Forward Europe*), and he died in 1964 before seeing the big nationalist successes towards which he had devoted the larger part of his life.

The reiteration of the SNP electoral policy of 1946 was linked to the policy of rejecting dual party membership. After 1946 it was not possible to be both a member of the SNP and a member of another political party. MacCormick in the pre-war era, attempting to preserve party unity, had compromised on this issue, but the hard core of the party in 1946 was in no mood for such compromises. The idea of dual membership was too close to the all-party approach. It diluted the loyalties of the membership, dissipated their energies, and provided a basis for conflict within the party. Increasingly the SNP was coming under pressure from the Scottish Convention, which threatened to take over the leadership of the nationalist movement, and they sought to emphasize the purity of their position and wholly dissociate themselves from the Convention approach. The decision was very much an ideological decision; it was not forced on the SNP and in the short run, due to the loss of membership it entailed, probably damaged the party. Given the number of candidates the SNP was able to put into the field, conflicts of loyalty were comparatively rare for the membership at the practical level of electioneering and voting. It was believed, though, that the future of the SNP depended on the existence of a hard-core of dedicated, single-minded nationalists rather than a mass of half-hearted members who could be relied on for no more than an annual subscription.

By 1947 the Scottish Convention was very much stronger than the SNP, and by 1950 the Covenant Association had totally eclipsed the SNP. Throughout the 1950s the SNP probably had an active membership that stayed around two thousand, while in Inverness and its environs alone the Covenant Association claimed between fifteen hundred and two thousand members in 1954. Robert McIntyre, indeed, giving evidence to the Royal Commission on behalf of the SNP, while claiming branches all over Scotland declined to give membership figures of the party. While any close links between the SNP and the Covenant Association were probably not possible – the policy and personality differences clearly being too great – the antagonism of the SNP towards the Covenant Association meant that it failed to take full advantage of the break-up of the all-party movement. Some of the funds that remained after the winding up of the Association went to the SNP, but very few members did. For example, Inverness was the last Covenant Association branch to be closed. Over £200 went to the SNP but less than 20 per cent of the membership. The Liberal Party was probably the main beneficiary after 1956.

The Scottish Covenant Association was a truly national organization. At its peak time it had branches throughout Scotland and because of the size of its membership was, compared with previous nationalist bodies, a wealthy organization. The *Scots Independent*, which in 1939 had become an SNP organ rather than being a forum for all nationalist opinion, remained with the SNP when the 1942 split occurred, Dr John MacDonald resigning the editorship. The paper was taken over by the hard-line faction on the war issue, MacDonald perhaps having rather undiplomatically published a letter suggesting that Douglas Young's health precluded him from war service in any case. The circulation of the *Scots Independent* had increased from one thousand in 1939, when the MacCormick faction gained control of it, to between three and five thousand in 1942 after which its circulation again declined. This was very much exceeded by the Covenant newsletter. The *Highlands and Islands Covenanter* alone exceeded three thousand, while there was also the newsletter and, after 1952, the *Southern Covenanter*, published by the Dumfries and District Associations. Actual figures are difficult to ascertain, since the Association publications were distributed free on demand, though a small subscription was requested if postal service was required.

For the few years of its existence the Covenant Association maintained a high level of activity. Week-end conferences and school, speakers' classes, and commissions of inquiry into facets of Scottish life such as transport, depopulation, housing, tourism and fisheries were organized. Coronation souvenirs were sold with the Queen's 'correct' title, and the Covenant issued its own gramophone records of Scottish dance music, while on the occasion of Burns's bi-centenary special stamps were sold by the Association, twenty for one shilling. Canvassers were trained and then organized to circulate the Association publications, bring in new members, collect signatures for the Scottish Covenant and later for the Scottish Declaration. On the social side balls, dances, whist drives, bazaars and ceilidhs had their place.

The problem facing the Covenant Association following the lack of interest displayed by both Attlee and Churchill in the response to the Scottish Covenant, was what to do next. While the Covenant had been a great propaganda success, it was clearly not a political weapon. The positions of the major political parties on the self-government issue had not noticeably changed and home rule seemed as far away as ever. The Association, in an attempt to maintain the momentum of the Movement, in 1952 circulated the Scottish Declaration, which read as follows:

I, the undersigned, believing that a Parliament in Scotland to deal with Scottish affairs is the first priority in Scottish politics, hereby pledge myself, irrespective of Party preference, to do everything in my power to secure the return to Parliament of Members who have promised the claims implicit in the Scottish Covenant.

In the event that I have no opportunity to help in the election of a candidate so committed, I declare that I shall withhold my support from any Government of the day which during its period of office has failed to take steps to secure the establishment of a Scottish Parliament within the framework of the United Kingdom.

I subscribe this pledge and make this declaration in the belief that the majority of Scottish Electors desire a measure of Self-Government, and that this desire will be achieved whenever a sufficient number of us demonstrate our willingness to put the interests of our country above those Party issues which have hitherto divided us.

The Scottish Declaration was not nearly as successful as the Scottish Covenant had been. It was not so well supported and neither did it generate the same degree of enthusiasm. Its timing also was wholly wrong. The Covenant Association published lists of marginal constituencies and attempted to estimate how many votes they could swing. But, with a General Election three years away, neither the parties nor individual Members of Parliament were going to get unduly perturbed. The Scottish Declaration also represented an admission by MacCormick that unless nationalism could move voters it would not be able to exert an influence on Parliament. Further, it also implied the end of the all-party approach, for had the Declaration been successful it would have been to the disadvantage of the Conservative Party, and in some constituencies the Labour Party, but would have benefited the Liberals everywhere.

The Covenant Association claimed successes, but in reality the Declaration was a failure. All it did was to demonstrate yet again that at the time party loyalties were stronger than national loyalties. Nationalism was not yet perceived as being relevant to the solution of Scottish problems.

D

In spite of the impressive organization it had developed and its frenetic activity, the Scottish Covenant Association arrived at a point where it had nowhere to go. The propaganda it had so brilliantly created was ignored by the Government and the public feeling it had aroused was successfully deflected by the Government's use of committees and commissions. The Association did not contest elections – although MacCormick had earlier contested Inverness for the Liberals in 1943 and then Paisley in 1948 with Conservative backing. John MacDonald, in fact, ended his political career by suggesting in the *Covenanter* in 1955 that the Association should contest elections. The point was that all the ceilidhs, parties, balls and whist drives would not serve to maintain an organization that had become aimless. A political party, however unsuccessful, has always before it the prospect of the next election, and this imposes at least some degree of unity and discipline upon the membership. It provides the party with a reason for its existence. But, with the failure of the Covenant and the Declaration, no such reason existed for the Association. It withered away, aided perhaps by the ill-health of its founder, John MacCormick.

Two further ventures associated with the Covenant Association were the removal of the Stone of Destiny from Westminster Abbey and John MacCormick's court case at which he asserted that the Queen's Scottish title was not Elizabeth II but Elizabeth I. He argued that Scotland and England had ceased to exist as separate geopolitical units at the Treaty of Union. The title of Queen Elizabeth II implied a continuity of the English state, which implied also the continuity of the Scottish state, which meant that for Scotland the Queen's correct title was Elizabeth I, since never before had there been an Elizabeth on the Scottish throne. MacCormick lost his case, but undoubtedly gained a moral victory. His action symbolized the strong feeling many Scots had that the Union, intended as a partnership, had left Scotland in a subordinate relationship. Instead of Scotland it was North England. Throughout Scotland the case caused a great deal of interest, although south of the border it caused some hilarity.

Conversely, Iain Hamilton's exploit in uplifting the Stone of Destiny from Westminster Abbey and, after a series of adventures worthy of an Alastair Maclean thriller, lodging it in Scotland, was treated far more seriously by the English authorities. Traditionally the Stone was used at the coronation of the Scottish kings and mythology has it that it was the stone upon which Jacob slept when he dreamed of the ladder to heaven. The Stone was taken from Scotland by the conqueror Edward I and never returned. Plans for its restoration to Scotland by unconventional means were laid by student nationalists of every generation. The possible methods of effecting its removal from Westminster Abbey were as well known among the interested fraternity as are the more theoretical routes to the top of Everest among mountaineers. The project was entirely successful, and for a while the Stone was hidden in a mason's yard in Glasgow. At an interview I had with a now middle-aged nationalist implicated in the affair, I was told that a number of replicas were made.

MacCormick was aware of the venture and instrumental in the return of the Stone to the authorities. The attitude of most nationalists, and probably of most Scots, was one of amusement not unmixed with a certain pleasure at the return of the Stone to Scotland. Fortunately the authorities, having blown the incident up out of all proportion, soft-pedalled on the legal proceedings for fear of creating martyrs.

The demise of the Covenant Association left the field clear to the SNP. The National Party did not, though, make much initial headway in spite of this freedom. It was not until the 1961 Bridgeton by-election that their fortunes took an upward turn. The 1955 and 1959 elections did little to strengthen nationalist morale or give hope for the future. After the Bridgeton by-election and the one in West Lothian the following year, however, nationalist prospects looked very different, and by 1968 the Party was the largest in Scotland.

In the next chapter we shall be considering some of the explanations that have been put forward to explain the phenomenal growth and success of the SNP. But what must be recognized is that the rise of nationalism in Scotland was intimately connected to changes in the *British* electorate. The Scottish situation soon developed a dynamic of its own, but it owed its initial success not to any particular Scottish causes but to the failure of the Labour and Conservative Parties to generate enthusiasm in the electorate. The fact that an opportunity occurred due to the workings of the British party system did not, however, in itself guarantee the success of the SNP. They have to be credited with making the most of a small opportunity. To understand how that opportunity came to be so readily accepted, it is necessary to take account of the history of nationalism, at least since 1928.

It is easy to over-estimate the continuity of the SNP as an organization before and after 1962. In many ways they were different parties. But in one important respect the SNP after West Lothian was dependent upon the party that was. By the end of the 1950s the SNP had resolved the major internal problems confronting it. The series of issues that had split the Party at various times were behind it. MacCormick's machinations in the late 1930s and the instigation of exclusive party membership in 1946 had reduced the basis for left–right conflict within the SNP. The experience of the second Scottish Home Rule Association, the SNP in the years prior to 1942, and the brief and glorious flight of the Scottish Covenant Association, had shown that the all-party approach was ineffective. The elimination of multiple party membership and moderate support meant that the fundamentalists had won the day as far as the degree of devolution was concerned. The Party was united in the quest for an independent Scotland. And, since 1946, the SNP has been developing social and economic policies that were thought appropriate to a post-independent Scotland.

It is unlikely that the SNP could have become a successful mass party had it faced the electorate in the state of disarray that had marked its early history. Unity and coherence of policy were not enough to guarantee the success of the SNP, but the Party would not have been successful had this not existed. Seen as an evolutionary process, the divisions, arguments, bitternesses and secessions so common within the nationalist movement played a role in preparing the SNP to make the most of the opportunity when it arose. Perhaps the nationalists were lucky as far as timing was concerned, for they were barely ready when that opportunity occurred.

CHAPTER SIX

Explaining the Growth of Scottish Nationalism

It was suggested previously that national feeling is a permanent feature of Scottish culture. It is not possible, therefore, to explain the rise of a nationalist movement by referring to a sudden spread of nationalist sentiment. What is needed is an explanation of why the nationalist feelings already held by many Scots became politicized when they did. Why not in 1928, or in 1945? Explicitly nationalist organizations have existed since 1853, but only in 1961 did the Movement begin to suggest that it might disrupt the political system. So any adequate explanation must cope with this question of timing above all.

In the natural sciences the notion of explanation is relatively simple compared to that held in the social sciences. Something is said to be 'explained' when it is found to be covered by a general law and is congruent with an accepted scientific theory. In social science, though, general laws are rare and their existence controversial; usually the best that can be achieved are statistical generalizations. To complicate matters, there are few accepted theories in social science; most are the subject of hot debate. A further problem is that while different explanations for a phenomenon may be complementary, it is often difficult to establish linkages between them. The same event may be looked at from an economic, a psychological, a political, an anthropological or a sociological point of view. It is often difficult to see how the different explanations can be fitted together since their central concepts do not necessarily overlap.

Yet, in spite of these difficulties, social scientists accept as a working maxim that the most general theory should be sought. So an explanation that is applicable to the rise of protest parties in Denmark, Basque nationalism in Spain and urban ghetto riots in the United States, as well as to the growth of Scottish nationalism, is to be preferred to an explanation that treats each of these as unique historical sequences. The aim is always to discover what is common to each apparently unique situation.

Laudable though this aim is, we shall see that the generalizing approach has not really been successful in explaining Scottish nationalism. At best three general explanations that will be examined can only be considered as very partial and, at worst, as wrong. But, while general explanations at the moment appear inadequate, explanations that are restricted in scope to the British situation seem to provide more enlightenment about the causes of the rise in political nationalism. The ubiquitous 'protest vote' will be considered, as well as 'relative deprivation' and 'colonial' explanations, but finally we must also consider a 'British' explanation.

THE PROTEST VOTE

Perhaps the most popular explanation of the rise in SNP parliamentary strength is that it is due to protest voting. The notion of the protest vote has in political science a fairly specific meaning. Many voters have what is termed a 'party identification', that is, they feel closer to one party and normally vote for that party; sometimes, however, they will feel dissatisfied with the performance of that party and will vote against it.

There are a number of points that need to be made about the protest vote. Firstly, it is usually seen as being a response to economic conditions. In Scotland in the middle and late 1960s unemployment was unacceptably high and, in spite of Government promises, it did not appear to be lessening. Labour voters, it is argued, defected to the SNP 'to teach Labour a lesson'. Also, it is the third or fourth parties that benefit from the protest vote rather than the major opposition party. In Scotland it is the Liberal Party or the SNP who would benefit directly by Labour defection rather than the Conservative Party: the psychological step from Labour to Conservative or vice versa is too large for most people. In addition, a protest vote usually occurs when there is little damage to the party the defector is protesting against. This means in effect that it is a by-election and local election phenomenon. At a general election there is the serious business of electing a Government, and it is usually important to the elector neither to waste his vote on a negative gesture nor to vote in such a way that he lets the opposition in. Following from this, the protest vote is only a temporary defection which will mean that the vote for the third and fourth parties will fluctuate wildly, registering highs between general elections and evaporating when they are held. Another feature is that the protest vote usually manifests itself against a party in power. Opposition parties, due to their lack of responsibility, do not get blamed in the same way that governing parties do. The voter assumes that the latter ought to be able to rectify the situation, so only those with the capability to act normally get the blame. Lastly, the protest vote is essentially a negative vote. It is a vote against rather than for something. It is the voter's expression of discontent with his home party rather than a positive affirmation of his agreement with the policy of his temporary party.

The protest vote explanation is popular because it does appear to cover some of the facts. In the period between 1966 and 1970 the nationalists seemed to achieve a remarkable breakthrough. They did well in the Pollok by-election and in 1967 won Hamilton, a Labour stronghold, at a by-election. In the 1968 municipal elections they also did extremely well. In spite of these successes, however, the nationalist vote at the 1970 general election was only 11 per cent. Although this was more than double their 1966 percentage of the Scottish vote, it was achieved by fielding sixty-five candidates as against only twenty-three in 1966. In real terms this represented a decrease of 16 per cent in the number of votes per candidate. In addition the party membership, which was only around 2,000 in 1962, was said to be as large as 120,000 in 1968, a peak from which it declined to around 70,000 in 1971. These facts, taken together, fitted the protest vote quite well.

While there is undoubtedly an element of truth in the protest vote explanation, there are good reasons for rejecting it. At best it would only be a contributory factor in the development of the SNP, for on this view it is difficult to account for the rise of the SNP rather than the Liberal Party. In fact, as we shall see, the Liberal Party did benefit, but given the years of comparative failure behind it, why was it that the nationalists should begin to succeed at that particular time? After the two 1974 general elections it was generally recognized that the protest view is inadequate, even though it still has its adherents today.

Basically, there were four errors made in putting forward this view. Firstly, it was not recognized that, if sustained protest voting were to occur, this would itself change the political situation in Scotland. A reasonable case can be made out that for many years a substantial body of opinion in Scotland desired some form of devolution. The Beaverbrook straw poll of 1932, the Kirriemuir Plebiscite of 1949, and the success of the Scottish Covenant Association in the early 1950s would all seem to attest to this. Devolution had not become a political issue because neither of the two major political parties wished to adopt the issue and because for most voters it was fairly low on their list of political priorities. However, a substantial shift of voters from the major parties to the SNP gives rise to the possibility of an electoral voice for nationalism: a vote for the nationalists is no longer seen as a wasted vote, and it becomes more attractive to those with only a slight party identification or with no party attachment at all. Further, it brings the question of devolution to the forefront of politics. Thus, in certain circumstances a protest vote can give rise to a chain reaction.

Secondly, while the protest explanation attempts to link events in Scotland to events in England (a perfectly justifiable procedure) what it failed to recognize was that there were factors in the Scottish situation that made it very different from the English one. For example, there is and always has been a very strong sense of Scottish identity that has no counterpart in the English situation, and which the SNP was able to tap. Further, there is in Scotland a separate media system which concentrated upon Scottish affairs and thus gave the SNP a great deal more publicity than, say, the Liberals got in England. In Scotland the nationalists have always been good news; from the early 1960s they began to become serious news.

Thirdly, the protest explanation did not allow for changes and developments within the SNP. It tended to treat the SNP as the effect of events outside it, rather than recognizing that the SNP was itself a cause of some of its own success. The SNP between 1966 and 1970 successfully made the transition from being a small, loosely coordinated organization to a mass political party, albeit with a very decentralized organizational structure. Although the leadership of the SNP had frequently been denigrated, they do have some leaders at local and national level of a stature equal to that of other parties. Also the party has learned how to use the mass media to effect and how to play the propaganda game.

Lastly, overmuch reliance upon voting statistics, especially in so short a period, tends to miss the deeper trends. Electoral statistics are, in any case, only meaningful in relation to the context in which they are found; the protest vote view ignores this context and risks misinterpreting the data.

One reason for the popularity of the protest vote explanation was that it was based upon wholly unrealistic expectations concerning the performance of the SNP in the 1970 general election. Many commentators merely extrapolated from the SNP's 1967 and 1968 successes to the 1970 general election, and when they found that the SNP vote had not held up they concluded that the nationalist bubble had burst. For several reasons this was far too premature a view; the ability of the SNP to draft large numbers of canvassers into a constituency is legendary. While this is possible in a by-election or in a general election where only a few candidates are standing, it is more difficult when all or nearly all the seats are being contested. Thus, in the 1970 general election the SNP organization was strained to breaking point. Further, it should be remembered that in 1966 most of the contested seats were selected because they offered the possibility of some success. In 1970 this was not the case; the SNP, in order to become a nation-wide political party, was forced to contest seats in very unfavourable constituencies where they had little or no chance. In 1966 only 43 per cent of the candidates standing lost their deposits, while in 1970 over two-thirds of them suffered this ignominy. In 1970, whether an effective constituency organization existed or not, the seat was contested and with lamentable consequences.

To some extent the SNP organization had suffered through their successes in 1968. Many of their most able local leaders were engaged in council work which left them little time to devote to party business. In addition, in making a bid to become a truly national party, the SNP had to abandon the emphasis that it had formerly placed upon local issues in elections. In municipal elections and even by-elections candidates were able to act in chameleon fashion, and could on many issues adopt a stance that most favoured their election, but by 1970 this was no longer possible. While the party remained organizationally decentralized, there was a movement towards ideological centralization. Through their greater exposure on the mass media the leadership was gaining greater control over the policy stance of the party, and the lesser degree of local adaptability now possible meant that candidates to a greater extent had to toe the party line. The electorate generally were more aware of what the party line was, and this in itself tended to discourage some voters from voting SNP.

Another factor that increased the plausibility of the protest vote was the fact that between 1968 and 1971 there appeared to be a massive decline in the membership of the SNP, the loss seeming to be somewhere in the region of 50,000. In fact, it is probable that the figures themselves are wrong. The membership figure of 120,000 usually given for 1968 was based upon the cards issued by SNP headquarters to the branches and not the number of cards issued by the branches to subscribing members. Membership figures are in any case only weak indicators of a party's strength. What really matters is how many of those members are active, as against being merely subscription members. And there is some reason to believe that since 1968 the ratio of active to passive members has increased. If this is the case, then the SNP is actually stronger at grass-roots level even though it has fewer members.

Most importantly, though, between 1968 and 1970 the SNP became the principal target for attack from all sides. Each major party attempted to prevent SNP recruitment among its own followers by labelling the SNP with the attributes of the opposition party. Thus Labour typified nationalists as 'Tartan Tories', while the Conservatives attempted to brand the SNP with a left-wing image. Further, there was an attempt by the two major parties to refuse to take the nationalists seriously, to drown them in ridicule, elements of which can still be discerned today. In addition, both Labour and Conservatives attempted to steal the nationalists' clothes. In 1968 Edward Heath as Prime Minister suggested that some form of devolution might not come amiss in Scotland, and set up a committee headed by Lord Home to inquire into the matter. The Labour Government, on the other hand, set up a Royal Commission, a time-honoured method of appearing to act. This turned out to be a political time-bomb with a slow-burning fuse.

Between 1966 and 1970, then, the SNP became a well-organized mass political party. Its success was to survive with credibility intact, having fought the 1970 general election on a national front. The degree of fluctuation that seemed to mark the SNP surge as a protest vote was more apparent than real, and there were very good reasons why it did not achieve greater success. In an electoral system that is heavily weighted against third and fourth parties, the SNP had managed to break into that system: 11·4 per cent of the Scottish vote is not an insignificant number of votes, and it was more than sufficient to maintain party confidence.

It is also difficult to argue that defections to the SNP have in the main been of a temporary nature. Of those changing their party and voting SNP around 70 per cent have stayed with the SNP, so for many the change is permanent. In the eyes of many voters, perhaps of all political persuasions, the SNP is good for Scotland. Many people are aware that it is only since the SNP achieved its successes that the plight of Scotland has become a central political issue. A substantial majority of Labour, Liberal and Conservative voters believe this, and it would appear to indicate that there may be a considerable reservoir of potential support for the SNP which is as yet untapped. The SNP has injected into Scottish political life, and possibly British political life, a vitality, interest and excitement that was not present before.

Electoral changes, though, do not occur only through people changing their political party. In the long term this is often one of the less important factors. Change can also occur through the political attachments of people newly entering the political system. In the mid-1960s the SNP managed to mobilize many people who had not previously voted, or who had no permanent party identification. More importantly, the party has for some years been disproportionately gaining the allegiance of new and young voters. One of the most important findings of political science is that voting has a reinforcing effect. The longer an individual has been loyal to and voted for a political party, the less probability there is that he or she will change. Also, it has been discovered that there is a high probability that the party that the individual first supports will be a permanent choice. These are only tendencies, for at times a critical election occurs when large numbers of voters may change. This was the situation after the First World War in Britain, and in America in the 1930s. What is striking about the Scottish situation is that nearly half of these voters between the ages of eighteen and thirty-four declare for the SNP, compared with around 20 per cent for Labour and Conservative.

Considerations such as these lead to two conclusions. Firstly, that the change in the Scottish political system is a permanent realignment of political forces. Support for the SNP will not just fade away as would be the case were it just a protest vote. Secondly, that it is likely to increase, due both to further defections and through the influx of young voters. This conclusion will be further reinforced when, in Chapter Eight, we consider the tactical position of the SNP in a future Scottish Assembly.

A further mark of the protest vote is that it is essentially against rather than for something. In the case of the SNP this is difficult to argue since there is a high degree of congruence between SNP aims on the devolution issue and what the SNP voter wants. A high level of voter/party congruence on most policy issues is comparatively rare, but around 85 per cent of SNP voters want either a new political system in Scotland or independence, the latter being the SNP position. On the devolution issue the SNP represents its supporters far more fully than do the Conservative or Labour parties.

The convergence in views between the SNP and the nationalist voter appears to have developed since the mid-1960s when there was a fairly wide difference between them. This movement perhaps reflects what has been happening more generally to Scottish public opinion: the SNP have not moved their position, but public opinion has been gently moving in its direction. Even among Conservative and Labour voters there is considerable support for extensive devolution or even independence, and the emergence of the Scottish Labour Party is perhaps evidence of this. It would be presumptuous to assume that this process has as yet been halted; given the benefits that so many Scots see as flowing from the demand for devolution, it may be the case that there is a long way to go yet.

THE RELATIVE DEPRIVATION EXPLANATION

Like many social scientific terms, 'relative deprivation' has become common in everyday use. Radio and television pundits, along with newspaper and periodical commentators, use and misuse the term with gay abandon; but in social science there is a fairly specific meaning. As early as the beginning of the nineteenth century it was recognized that civil discontent often did not manifest itself among those who appeared to be most deprived; the most dissatisfied sections of society were frequently those who were comparatively well-off. The theory of relative deprivation was created to attempt to explain this.

Industrial society is a vast network of relationships and most of us exist only within a small niche and interact with a comparatively small number of other people. Our jobs, hobbies, interests, education, where we live, and our position in the social hierarchy necessarily limit the number and type of people with whom we interact on a regular basis. And, just as our interactions with other people are limited, so are the people and groups with whom we compare ourselves. The degree of deprivation we feel is relative only to these, not to any absolute standard. Thus, a person may be poorest of the poor and yet not feel relatively deprived, because he feels his position just and those he compares himself with are also poor. Another person, although fairly affluent, feels deprived because he compares himself with a social group which has, perhaps, higher status.

The relative deprivation explanation for the rise of Scottish nationalism goes something like this. Since the late 1950s there has developed in Scotland a sense of relative deprivation with respect to England, especially South East England, and some of the smaller European states. Harold Macmillan told the British peoples 'You have never had it so good', which may have been true of South East England, but did not seem to apply to the industrial heartland of Scotland, where unemployment remained unacceptably high, the rate of emigration did not lessen, and the standard of housing remained abysmally low. While the economy of the South East boomed, most of Scotland became a development area with the traditional heavy industries declining and new industries not growing fast enough to replace them. In addition, the advent of commercial television was a shop window for expensive commodities which everyone saw but few people were able to buy.

Later the British economy as a whole began to suffer from the same malaise that had long affected Scotland. The Scots looked at some of the small European states – Sweden, Norway, Iceland, Denmark, Finland – and saw how well they were doing and how rapidly their standard of living was increasing, while Scotland remained a stagnant economy. It did not seem just to many Scots that the South East of England should be so wealthy and Scotland so poor, and neither did it seem right that Scotland should sink further while countries elsewhere, no richer than Scotland in natural or population resources, should exhibit strong economic growth. Nationalism, so this argument runs, is the Scottish answer. The SNP represents a way forward that old-style party politics could not guarantee.

This is a very plausible theory and undoubtedly it makes a great deal of sense, especially in the light of statements made by the SNP leadership. As an explanation of why most people vote for the SNP, as opposed to becoming activist nationalists, it seems wrong. Perhaps, to be entirely fair, we should conclude that the case is not proven from two points of view. Firstly, while the concept of relative deprivation appears on the surface to be fairly straightforward, in reality it is a very complex notion with a number of associated theoretical problems that do not seem to have been taken into account in this case. Secondly, what empirical evidence there is (and this is fairly scanty) does not give unambiguous results. If anything, it argues against a relative deprivation theory.

There are three theoretical points we will make here, but these should be sufficient to display the inadequacy of any simple theory of relative deprivation. Firstly, people may feel deprived in a number of different ways: they may be economically deprived, in that their income is not what they feel it ought to be; or they may feel deprived in terms of social welfare values – housing, health facilities or education; or they may feel deprived politically, believing that they or the group to which they belong are not being given an opportunity to influence political decisions; again, they may feel status deprivation – that they are not valued sufficiently by society for what they are, or what they do. This variety in the way that people can feel deprived would not matter if all types of felt deprivation had the same sort of effect upon political behaviour. But numerous studies have shown this not to be the case. Sometimes a sense of deprivation can lead to resignation or quiescence, rather than to political activism. One factor affecting this is whether people feel they have a right to the things of which they feel deprived. What this means in practice is that there is no easy connection between relative deprivation and the development of radical politics. It will depend upon how intensely people feel deprived, what they are deprived of, how long they are deprived of it, and whether their sense of social justice tells them they ought to have it.

Secondly, if a sense of relative deprivation is to be effective in motivating people politically, there must be opportunity for its expression. To take an extreme case, in a repressive police state no matter how deprived a person may feel, the barrel of a gun would normally serve as a sufficient disincentive to express it. At a less melodramatic level, there is a communication process involved. An isolated individual may feel deprived but is unlikely to do anything about it unless he is aware of a substantial body of support. The more support that people have in their opinions the more sure and confident they are in expressing them. And, before discontent becomes politically important, it is usually necessary for it to be focused upon a single cause for that discontent. If all those people who feel deprived put the blame in different places – on God, on the Jews, the Russians, the English, the ruling class, etc. – it would be difficult to get any concerted action to rectify the perceived ill. Usually an organization is necessary to pull together the existing discontent, to give it rational justification and to devise a programme of action designed to alleviate the discontent. What this means is that a sense of relative deprivation can only in a partial sense be the 'cause' of a social movement. Many other things are also necessary before it can become a politically important factor.

These two points have stressed that there is no straightforward connection between relative deprivation and the emergence of a social movement. Now we must question the assumption that a widespread sense of relative deprivation is really necessary for this emergence. What is being suggested is that political nationalism may be caused by active Scottish nationalists and, as all revolutionary propaganda seeks to change the public's frame of reference, to provide aspirations and possibilities that were previously unthought of, and to make these seem realistic and attainable, it also usually provides a means of attaining these ends. Rather than treating nationalism wholly as the result of social conditions and the effect these conditions have upon public perceptions, to some extent these perceptions may be seen as the successful outcome of attempts to convince a large section of the Scottish voting public that the SNP is a credible alternative. We shall return to this point later.

In effect these three points mean that were we to discover a high relationship between nationalist voting and relative deprivation, the relative deprivation theory would still be somewhat ambiguous and open to a number of interpretations. Further, given the survey evidence available, it is not possible to estimate the degree of change that has occurred in the perceptual framework of people in Scotland. The relative deprivation explanation can only be sustained if it can be shown either that there is a change in the intensity with which deprivation is felt, or that it is the framework itself that has changed. There are no overtime data to support either view. Rather, it may just be the case that the Scottish public, because of the failure of the two major parties to achieve desired ends, has turned to the nationalists as an alternative means. Previously, faith in the Labour and Conservative Parties kept most Scottish voters from voting nationalist, but the loss of faith opened the way for SNP success.

A number of studies have looked at relative deprivation in a Scottish context, and the conclusion must be that the results are ambiguous and somewhat puzzling. A sample survey in Glasgow discovered that a sense of relative economic deprivation vis-à-vis the English was totally unrelated to SNP voting. This finding was confirmed in a mass sample survey in the late 1960s which covered the whole of Scotland. In neither did it appear that a sense of life-style deprivation was related to SNP voting, although a sense of occupational deprivation was weakly related. Strangely, though, the two big SNP surges, in 1967–8 and 1974, both occurred when the unemployment figures were not too bad, at least by historical standards, at slightly under and slightly over 4 per cent. The most important finding was that there is a strong relationship between a sense of political deprivation and SNP voting.

These findings present us with something of a problem. Since the 1930s the nationalist movement in Scotland has been growing steadily more pragmatic. During and prior to the 1930s nationalism was strongly associated with a desire for cultural revival. Great emphasis was laid on the distinctive dialects of Scotland, Scottish history, dance, song and the ancient symbols of Scotland. In the quest for a credible and realistic political image, the SNP has de-emphasized these aspects of the nationalist movement, although they still play a small part. The SNP did not wish to be branded as romantics or idealists, but wanted to appear as practical men and women with a workable alternative for Scotland's future. Plaid Cymru, the Welsh nationalist party, on the other hand, has maintained a high level of cultural content, especially with regard to the language issue. The SNP appeal, rather, has been framed in economic terms. The major argument has been that Scottish political control is necessary to halt the deterioration of the Scottish economy, and this message has been hammered home as often as possible by pointing to the various economic ills that beset Scotland. But it seems that, while the SNP on the public platform have appeared to have great success in their arguments against the spokesmen of other parties, their economic arguments have not been a major element in motivating the public to vote for the SNP. Rather, it is a perception of political deprivation that is important to people, a far more difficult case to sustain. It could, perhaps, be argued that the Scottish public have merely skipped the intervening arguments in the overall case for political control.

To conclude this section, we must reiterate that plausible though the relative deprivation theory first appears, it is difficult to accept it as an explanation of the rise in Scottish nationalism. Most of those who have proposed this as an explanation have, in any case, been referring to economic and welfare deprivation which is clearly incorrect. If the explanation has any validity whatsoever it is with regard to a feeling of political deprivation, and it is difficult to know whether this is a cause or an effect in the final analysis.

THE COLONIAL EXPLANATIONS

There are two explanations of the rise of political nationalism in Scotland that make references to colonialism. The will be referred to as the 'decline of Empire' thesis and the 'internal colonialism' thesis. Although they are occasionally linked together, for the purposes of analysis they will here be treated separately. When they are linked together, this is by seeing Scottish and Welsh nationalism as part of a continuing process of decolonization that began, most significantly, with the granting of Indian independence. Since then the wind of change has heralded in a new era of militant nationalism that has included some minority cultures within multinational states, as well as the better known examples of Third World nationalism. However, the decline of Empire thesis assumes the internal colonial thesis and in the case of Scotland the latter is dubious. Before Scottish nationalism can be seen as the latest and ultimate expression of the collapse of English colonialism, it has to be established that England and Scotland exist in a colonial relationship. There are good reasons for doubting this to be the case, although perhaps the argument has more validity regarding other parts of the United Kingdom with minority cultures.

The Decline of Empire Thesis gains its plausibility by the coherent pattern it imposes upon an historical sequence, and the way it seeks to link political changes within Britain to changes in the world position of the UK. The explanation rests upon two sets of related factors; that Britain's waning international position has certain psychological effects upon the cultural minorities in Britain, and that the loss of Empire has an effect upon the social structure of the minority cultures. Both of these effects have yet to be empirically demonstrated to general satisfaction.

In an earlier chapter it was suggested that, in a perverse way, the Union with England can be seen as an expression of nationalism, since participation in England's colonial trade was seen as the only way of ensuring Scotland's national development. Scotland after the Union became part of the most power-ful and wealthy society the world had till then seen, the masters of an Empire. The bargain seemed a good one. The sublimation of the Scottish identity in favour of a British identity and the right of self-determination in favour of joint determination were the costs that Scotland paid for the benefits that flowed from the Union.

With the decline of Empire, however, the benefits of a has-tily-donned British identity as opposed to a specifically Scottish identity became more questionable. Through the twentieth cen-tury Britain was gradually forced back into her native islands, ceding her overseas territories to the native populations and her world influence to those more capable of exercising it. Britain's days as a great power were over, although the old attitudes and illusions lingered on. The two super-powers dwarfed British pretensions to being a first-rate military power, as the Suez débâcle showed, and she also slipped down the economic league table. Many European nations attained growth rates which far surpassed that of Britain, and achieved standards of living undreamt of by the British. Bereft of the capacity to exploit the cheap labour and raw materials of the colonies, Britain was thrown back on her own resources and seemed destined to become the poor man of Europe. In an attempt to arrest the slide towards impoverishment, government increas-ingly intervened in the direction of the economy with a growth in bureaucracy and centralization and a resultant loss of control at local level.

Further, while Britain had an Empire to control and exploit, soldiers, administrators, farmers, planters, missionaries, adven-turers and pioneers were needed. For the ambitious and en-ergetic the colonies provided a means of achieving success that was not possible at home, as the rigid and hierarchical nature of British society, with its class divisions, made upward social mo-bility difficult. Those people who were most likely to be dis-sident troublemakers in other circumstances could make their own way by going into colonial service, but with the loss of Empire and the lack of opportunities at home the ambitious and energetic became increasingly frustrated and actively sought ways to change the situation. To cultural minorities the tie with England seemed more of a hindrance than a help to national progress, especially since the pride in being British was tinged with embarrassment. But they had another identity pre-pared, and it is to this that they now turned. Armed with the knowledge that small nations elsewhere were doing better, the cultural minorities in Britain came to see union with England as a block on national development.

But this explanation of Scottish nationalism fails on a number of grounds. As is common with grand, sweeping theory, the historical reality is distorted more than can be justified. While the theory attempts to explain the timing of recent political nationalism, it has a great deal of difficulty in accounting for past nationalistic activity. It should be remembered that it was due to a historical accident that Scotland did not get a federal assembly prior to 1920. In 1913 the issue appeared closed and was merely awaiting parliamentary time and the solution of the Irish question. Similarly, it would be difficult to fit militant Irish nationalism into any decline of Empire thesis for it existed long before there was evidence of decline. It seems fairly clear that the expression of militant nationalism in the British Isles is not dependent upon the well-being, existence or non-existence of a British Empire.

The fault of this type of theory is that the mere overlap of two historical sequences is taken as evidence that the one is causing the other. To take an absurd example, if the high summer temperatures in New York correlate with the death rate in China, it does not in any way mean that the former is causing the latter. It just means that the two sequences are oc-curring at the same time. If, however, linkages could be shown between the two sequences then we should feel more justified in relating them. Supposing that the heat energy emitted by this enormous metropolis set up air currents interfering with normal trade winds that affect rainfall and thus the rice crop in China, then we might wish to argue that high mortality in China was affected by high temperature in New York. The linkages provided between the decline of Empire and the rise of nationalism in Scotland are threefold: there is firstly the failure of the British economy due to its present inability to exploit its colonies; secondly, the frustration that occurs due to the lack of opportunity for social mobility in Britain; and thirdly, there is the decline among the cultural minorities of the British identity.

The relationship between economic success and colonial exploitation is a difficult one to establish. It is not at all clear that the employment of cheap or slave labour, especially if this is unskilled, is in the long run economically feasible. This is a well-trodden controversy in relation to the southern slave states of America prior to the civil war. Neither is it at all obvious that the absence of military colonialization means the end of economic exploitation by the wealthy industrialized nations among which the United Kingdom, despite her present difficulties, must be counted. Clearly physical occupation of underdeveloped territories is not necessary for economic success; if it were, we should be in difficulty explaining the economic successes of Japan, Germany, Sweden or Norway. Without going into the question more deeply, it is doubtful if the economic troubles that beset the United Kingdom are attributable to the fact that we no longer have a vast Empire.

The idea that Scottish nationalism arose due to the lack of opportunities elsewhere available to the ambitious and energetic, thus forcing them to stay at home and create their own opportunities, also seems very dubious. We would expect, if this were correct, that the SNP leadership would be frustrated, alienated and neurotic. This, however, appears to be wholly wrong. One study of SNP local leaders showed them to be as a group fairly well satisfied with their personal lot. Although much younger than their Labour or Conservative counterparts, they do not differ from them very much in terms of the type of job they hold or their social background. This also applies to the national leadership of the SNP, which is very much weighted towards the middle-class professional person. The local study also found that the local leaders were not demonstrably neurotic.

Furthermore, if this view were correct we might also expect a decline in the number of people emigrating from Scotland, and there appears to be little evidence for this. In fact, in 1965–6, the time immediately preceding the first series of SNP successes, the emigration rate actually increased to 47,000 people per year, while between 1961 and 1966 a total of 199,000 people emigrated. While the rate of emigration declined somewhat in the early 1970s, it remained by any standards very high.

Finally, the view that the sense of Britishness has declined to be replaced by a heightened sense of Scottishness does not appear plausible to anyone acquainted with Scottish history. It would be very difficult to sustain the view that being Scottish has ever been unimportant to Scots. The Scots have long had and been aware of a dual identity, and each identity was considered appropriate in different circumstances. What seems to have happened is that the Scottish identity has become relevant to politics, whereas previously politics was only seen in British terms. There may, in fact, be little mass change in the ordering or strength of either identity. The cause of the changed relevance of Scottishness to politics is probably due to changes in British society, and in the Labour and Conservative Parties, rather than in Scots themselves.

As we shall later argue, after 1959 the two major parties failed to fire the enthusiasm of the British electorate. In Scotland the SNP was able to take advantage of the vacuum left by the major parties and cause a permanent realignment of Scottish politics. They were able to take advantage of the alternative Scottish identity and make it politically relevant, while the Labour and Conservative Parties were still attempting to mobilize the electorate with appeals based on social class. Since 1974, though, the situation may have again changed. Due to the great success of the SNP in the two general elections of 1974, and their now central position in Scottish political life, they may have had the effect of heightening and intensifying this self-image of Scotland. This would of course be an effect of their success, rather than a cause.

The Internal Colonialism Thesis is another side of the colonial explanation. Normally we consider a colonial situation to exist when a rich advanced nation occupies an under-developed country with an aim to exploiting its resources. Usually the colonized country was in what we now refer to as the Third World, while the colonizing power was frequently a western European nation, such as Britain, Spain, Holland, Germany or France. In some situations, however, even within one state, a colonial situation may exist. Where there is a dominant ethnic group, usually a large majority, that group may exploit other ethnic groups within the state. That this is the case in Britain has been brilliantly argued by Michael Hechter in his book *Internal Colonialism: The Celtic Fringe in British National Development*, where he views the rise of militant nationalism in the UK as being the response of exploited cultures as they attempt to throw off their colonial shackles. According to Hechter an internal colonial situation may be said to exist when:

Commerce and trade among the members of the periphery tend to be monopolized by members of the core. Credit is similarly monopolized. When commercial prospects emerge, bankers, managers and entrepreneurs tend to be recruited from the core. The peripheral economy is forced into complementary development to the core, and thus becomes dependent upon external markets. Generally, this economy rests on a single primary export, either agricultural or mineral. The movement of peripheral labour is determined largely by forces exogenous to the periphery ... Economic dependence is reinforced through juridical, political and military measures. There is a relative lack of services, lower standard of living, and higher level of frustration ... There is national discrimination on the basis of language, religion, or other cultural forms. (p. 33)

Three points are relevant here. Firstly, it is not our argument that internal colonialism has not existed in Britain – for it surely has done – but that Scottish–English relations do not fit this framework. The thesis has considerable power as far as Ireland is concerned, but Scotland is in a completely different situation. Secondly, there is something of a problem in knowing when an

internal colonial situation exists. Of Hechter's nine conditions
that characterize an internal colonial situation, how many have
to exist in order for there to be internal colonialism? If, for
example, we found that discrimination existed with regard to
language, would we be justified in asserting that an internal
colonial situation existed? Or do all nine conditions have to be
present? Hechter recognizes this problem but defers the solution of it. Thirdly, even if the theory of internal colonialism is
correct, it cannot alone account for the timing of the nationalist
surge. It covers a period of some three hundred years, but only
in the last decade has nationalism in Scotland threatened the
unity of the UK. Hechter, in fact, utilizes a variant of relative
deprivation theory to bridge the gap between his historical
theory and the rise of political nationalism. But, as we have
already seen, there are severe problems with relative deprivation as an explanation.

Clearly, as even the casual visitor will recognize, Scotland is
in many ways very different from England. This does not mean,
however, that it is part of the 'Celtic fringe' in the same way
that Wales and Ireland are. In fact, Anglo-Saxon stock was as
native to Scotland as it is to England, settlement occurring
around the same time. Much of Scottish history can be seen in
the light of the Lowland and Highland cultures competing for
social and political dominance, with the Lowlanders achieving
their ultimate victory after 1745. Many of the symbols of Scotland today are of Celtic origin, but this was due to nineteenth-
century romanticism rather than to a genuine historical legacy.
Much the same can be said of Basque and Breton nationalism;
the history and significance of the past were rediscovered in the
nineteenth century and today provide a justification for the
claim to autonomy. What this means in the Scottish case is that
the type of cultural genocide that the English have, in Hechter's
view, been perpetrating upon the Scots, has just not occurred,
partly because the implied cultural chasm between the two
nations did not exist and partly because Scottish culture has
been institutionally protected. Over the past two and a half
centuries there has undoubtedly been assimilation; even the

law, although protected by the Treaty of Union, has moved closer to the English model. But much of what is called assimilation is, in fact, the result of the social demands of an industrial society. In the eternal search to maximize efficiency, and thereby productivity, similarities between nations as to their social organization will increase, particularly with the development of a world culture of ideas aided by instant communications. This does not mean, however, the end of nationalism. Nationalism, particularly twentieth-century nationalism, is most often a modernizing force and arises when a people seeks to become similar to those nations recognized as most advanced. While the myths of the past are the means of mobilizing the people, the aim is to modernize the country.

Of the conditions that Hechter considers to characterize internal colonialism many have little relevance to Scotland. Surely there is little or no discrimination on the basis of language or religion. Gaelic plays such a small role in Scottish nationalism that it can be considered as hardly an issue. While many, though by no means all, nationalist movements are based on linguistic distinctiveness – Welsh nationalism being a case in point – there is hardly any emphasis upon this in Scotland. From the formation of the NPS in 1928, linguistic factors have become steadily less important. With regard to religion, the Treaty of Union specifically protected the Kirk, although at the time of the Disruption in 1843 it was alleged that there was English interference. In general, though, religious discrimination against people belonging to the national church just has not occurred.

It is equally difficult to maintain that economic dependence is reinforced through juridical, political and military measures. The Scottish legal system was protected by the Treaty of Union; even so, due to the fact that Parliament does not recognize fundamental law (although it has been argued that the Treaty of Union constitutes an exception), the judiciary are constrained to implement parliamentary legislation. So, if there was evidence of inequitable legislation regarding Scotland in Parliament, this would be reflected in Scottish law. In fact, all

Scottish legislation is scrutinized by a Scottish committee and has to be passed separately from English legislation, although usually it is merely a Scottish equivalent.

Political measures could be taken against Scotland in one of two ways. Firstly, Scots could be denied political or social rights which are enjoyed by the English majority. This is not the case. There is no political right possessed by an Englishman that is not also possessed by those living in Scotland. It could even be argued that politically the Scots are in a better position than the English: on a population basis they are over-represented in Parliament. Many of the Government departments for the north of England are in distant Whitehall, while for Scotland they are located in Edinburgh, which perhaps allows better access to the official bureaucracy. Secondly, although Scots are over-represented compared with the English in Parliament, this would be of little importance if the English majority in Parliament was used to defeat the Scottish minority. In fact, though, until very recently Scots have elected MPs of the same parties as the English, and the basis of division in Parliament has been along party rather than regional lines. It could be argued in this respect that the Scots have been of recent years imposing their wishes on the English voter, since without the Scottish Labour vote England would have probably returned a majority of Conservative MPs fairly consistently. Only when English MPs combine as a bloc to vote against the united Scottish MPs can it be maintained that political measures are being taken against the Scots. And, until recently, there appeared no likelihood of this state of affairs arising.

Further, it is not usual for a colonized nation to provide the political leaders of the colonizing nation. Yet this frequently is what has happened in the United Kingdom. Since the Union there have been seven Scottish prime ministers and since 1900 Scotland has provided 9 per cent of British cabinet personnel, while Scots are very much over-represented in the higher reaches of the British civil service. Thus it is hard to find any sign of political or juridical oppression or discrimination on a racial basis, and impossible to find any indication of military repression. There has been no substantial military action in Scotland since 1745, and that was in part a case of Scot versus Scot.

Hechter's position regarding Scotland has rather more plausibility with economic factors, although even here his conclusions must be qualified. Obviously we must disagree with the proposition that Scotland is heavily dependent upon a single primary resource. She has a highly diversified industrial economy, no less so than that of England. On the other hand, there are areas of Scotland where the standard of living is unacceptably low, especially with regard to housing and particularly in Glasgow. Yet there is not a 'relative lack of services'. In fact, if the occupational structure of Scotland is compared to that of England, the remarkable thing is the extent of their similarity. In twenty-seven occupational categories the percentage of the population employed in each category is less than 2 per cent different for the two countries. Neither can we accept that in the Scottish situation dependence upon external markets is indicative of internal colonialism. As a small island with a large population to feed, Britain as a whole is similarly situated.

The serious side of Hechter's argument, though, revolves around the degree to which the Scottish economy is controlled from outside Scotland. For Scotland as a whole, only 41 per cent of manufacturing industry is internally controlled, while for the Clydeside conurbation this figure is somewhat higher. One of the long-term problems of the Scottish economy has been its over-dependence on shipbuilding and heavy industry in an era when there exists an international capacity for over-production in relation to demand. A similar problem is faced by the British car industry. So there has been a need to develop in Scotland new and more modern industries. The difficulty is that when these new light industries are introduced into the Scottish economy, they are nearly always externally controlled. The situation then arises that as the Scottish economy modernizes and becomes viable and competitive in the world markets, the ultimate control of the economy moves outside Scotland, either to elsewhere in the UK or, almost as importantly, to North America. Also, since the parent company is located elsewhere, there tends to be less emphasis upon research and development: this is generally done elsewhere and the results are made available for local branch industry. Further, in the days prior to tele-communications, the ability to make local decisions was limited even though financial control may have existed. But in a time of instant communication local autonomy is severely cir-cumscribed.

Within Scotland the movement of labour is heavily de-pendent upon external forces, although it should be noted that the high emigration rate experienced in Scotland is due rather to the lack of opportunity within Scotland. The unemployment rate within Scotland is always higher than the English rate; it is kept at its reasonably low level only by the constant exodus of young Scots, but the modernization of the Scottish economy has led to 'structural unemployment'. Although there may be jobs and opportunities in the newer industries, those people who have worked for many years in the older industries have not, without intensive re-training, the skills appropriate for the new industries. Thus there arises a mis-match between available jobs and available skills, with the resultant unemployment.

Three points need to be made regarding economic de-pendency and the internal colonial thesis. Firstly, the relationship between economic and political control is a very controversial one. Political scientists, economists and sociolog-ists have been arguing about this issue for at least a century. The issue is sufficiently questionable to make one wonder whether, if the SNP did gain control of Scotland and set up an autonomous state, they would be able to affect the degree of external control of the Scottish economy without severely dam-aging the standard of living. This is a criticism of SNP aims which is voiced by the Scottish Council of the Labour Party and which merits serious consideration. Hechter, though, considers that the Scottish situation can be changed by political means within a United Kingdom framework. Secondly, in time econ-omic penetration of the economies of other nations may become an inadequate criterion for deciding whether internal colonialism exists. At the moment economic relationships are often so one-sided as to prejudice one of the partners' chances of gain. But, more and more within organized groups of nations, economic interpenetration is becoming acceptable, especially when this brings investment. A real problem is caused by the emergence over the past few decades of the multinational company, which owes allegiance only to itself and, due to its amorphous nature, is difficult to control.

Finally, while on many points we have to reject Hechter's thesis, it does appear to have validity with regard to economic factors in recent times. With attempts to modernize the Scottish economy external control has increased, but there is little need to take a three-hundred-year time span for this thesis. De facto political control began to be exerted on Scotland with the increase in communications which began in the middle and late nineteenth century, and which was matched by increased administrative decentralization. External economic control is a phenomenon that began after the First World War and since the Second World War has continued at an increasing rate. However, in order to relate the internal colonial thesis to the rise of nationalism, linkages are again required. For a mass movement such as the SNP we need to be able to relate the actions of the voter to the economic facts he or she perceives. Such a linkage has not been empirically demonstrated, which makes it difficult to conceive of internal colonialism as a cause of the rise in nationalism.

THE BRITISH EXPLANATION

Scottish nationalism differs mainly from other post-war European minority nationalisms in the degree of its success. Undoubtedly it does have some similarities with other resurgent European nationalisms, but the reasons for its success are to be found in circumstances peculiar to Britain. By taking notice of the situation in Britain it becomes possible to see why Scottish nationalism became such a potent political force when it did. In outline, the SNP became a viable political party because the two major parties lost the allegiance of a significant number of voters. The SNP did not in any way create the circumstances in which they could be successful, but with considerable energy, skill and enterprise they took advantage of those circumstances. The decline of partisanship within the electorate was general throughout Britain, but because of historical factors, social developments, and the activity of the SNP, it had implications for Scotland that were hardly evident in England and were not so profound in Wales.

One of the most irritating facts for nationalists was that they had, since 1928, received 'infinitely more sympathy than votes'. The problem was that it appeared impossible to translate the desire of most Scots for greater autonomy into political power. As an issue it remained low on the list of public priorities. A hint of what was necessary to achieve this translation was given during the war years, when in a time of electoral truce between the major parties, the SNP achieved some striking by-election results. When there was a breakdown in normal party competition the SNP did well, but when the major parties used all the means at their disposal to rally the faithful, the SNP challenge failed. Two things aided the SNP at these and later by-elections. Firstly, by-elections are conducted in a freer and less structured political atmosphere than are general elections. They are not considered so important from a national point of view, and thus issues can be given a hearing which would be lost in the noise of a general election. The major parties in a general election campaign define the important issues and their leaders receive the lion's share of available media coverage. Their attempts to bring attention to other public issues are lost in the thunder of major party confrontation. Secondly, when competition between the major parties lessens there are more free voters of different persuasions available who can unite under the nationalist banner. It is a fact that in Scotland very few people feel antagonistic to the SNP – even firm adherents of other parties in the main believe that the SNP have done a lot of good for Scotland – and when old party loyalties erode, the SNP is psychologically easy for the Scottish voter to choose.

In the 1945 general election the Labour Party achieved a large majority and proceeded to give effect to policies deemed wholly unacceptable to the Conservative opposition. There was little that the Conservatives could do about it, but political tempers ran high. It was the first time that the Labour Party had gained a clear parliamentary majority, and this seriously shook the Conservative belief in their divine right to rule – that they were the natural party of government. The turn-out in the 1945 general election was low, but this had nothing to do with the lack of political conflict. It was due to the fact that because of the war the electoral register had not been updated, with the result that large numbers of people were disenfranchised. In the general elections of 1950 and 1951 turn-out was higher than it has been at any subsequent general election.

The turn-out at general elections is an important statistic. It can indicate, though only in very rough terms, the extent to which the electorate considers the issues discussed in an election important. Other things affect turn-out also, but it is a general indicator of the degree of partisanship that exists within the electorate. If the political parties are not able to inspire enthusiasm among the voting public for either the party or the cause, then the voter will stay at home on polling day. In Scotland in 1951 81·2 per cent of those entitled to vote did so, while in 1955 this dropped to 75·1 per cent. While it fluctuated between these two figures at intervening general elections, in 1970 the turn-out in Scotland was only 74 per cent, while in England it was as low as 71·3 per cent. Further, while the two major parties retained their grip on the House of Commons, largely due to the workings of the British electoral system which advantages the larger parties, their share of the vote dropped. This is not the same thing as saying that the votes of the SNP rose, for the finding was British rather than merely Scottish. In both England and Scotland the Liberal share of the vote did rise, though this was not reflected in the number of seats they gained.

The difference was that in Scotland it was possible, given the vacuum in political enthusiasm that existed, for the underlying dimension of nationalism to be politically mobilized. Given a small foothold in the electoral system, by dint of hard work and organization, with a degree of good fortune over the discovery of oil, the SNP consolidated their position. The Liberal Party in England, however, could not maintain their early momentum. They were not able to appeal to the English electorate on so salient an issue as home rule and were forced to remain in the political mould cast by the major parties. In Scotland, the obvious benefits that flowed to Scotland following the 1970 election results persuaded many people that, even if they did not support the idea of independence, a vote for the SNP would 'do a lot of good for Scotland'. The two major parties were, however, split on the question of home rule, only the Liberal Party presenting a unified policy as they had done for many years.

Further evidence that the SNP did not create their opportunity but merely took advantage of a political opening can be shown by looking at the constituencies where the SNP have done particularly well. While the SNP breakthroughs in many constituencies appeared very sudden, in reality there was considerable continuity. The two-party dominance was being challenged before the SNP became politically significant, in many cases as far back as 1959. In 1959 and 1964, for example, in Angus (South) the Liberal Party did well, before their activity in disturbing the two-party system was taken over by the SNP in 1970 and 1974. A similar tendency can be found elsewhere, in Argyll, Banff, and Galloway, for example, among Conservative-held seats, while in Labour seats such as the Western Isles there was a similar trend. In Labour-held seats where the SNP have done well, they have tended to attack directly rather than take advantage of the disequilibrium created by a Liberal incursion.

Why should the chance arise for the SNP in the 1960s? There were a number of contributory factors. From 1955 onwards the Conservative and Labour Parties moved very much closer together: it was the era of 'Butskellism' when the moderates of both parties found they had much in common. The Conservative Party, presided over by the benign and paternal

Harold Macmillan, had by the end of the 1960s lost much of its impetus and had no real policies to follow. This was shown, perhaps, by the Conservative Government's economic policy. The Labour leadership had created by their moderation a gap between themselves and the traditional activists, and the Labour Party conferences became occasions for ritual blood-letting. The election of Harold Wilson to the leadership, an erstwhile radical, staunched the flow. In 1966 he promised the country a new future based upon a modernized society, but the new technological revolution failed to materialize. Perhaps the most important development in this era was the emergence of the Common Market debate, but the parties were divided within themselves on this. Basically, there was a lack of direction in the politics of the day, perhaps even a failure of leadership. In some ways the rapid spread of television acted to reduce the prestige of political leaders. It brought current debates into the home, and these were often petty and more concerned with debating points and party politics than issues, and politicians were seen to be very fallible mortals rather than wise and statesmanlike figures. Into this dreary scene the SNP burst, enthusiastic, voluble, ambitious and positive. They might well be lunatics but at least they knew what they wanted. And slowly, partly because of the quality of some of their personnel, they gained a more favourable image and achieved a few good results, starting the snowball that would gather pace particularly after 1970. But the basis for this success was laid both before and after 1961.

The success of nationalism in Scotland, though, was not due solely to the arrival of an electoral opportunity caused by the electorate's disillusion. This merely created space which might have been exploited just as successfully by the Liberal Party as it was by the SNP. Thus, while political disillusionment loosened the attachment of many voters to their parties, the SNP had to be capable of taking advantage of the situation, and the political activity of the SNP was a crucial factor in the rise of nationalism. Some social theories tend to assume an automatic linkage between the emergence of a social movement and the social conditions that foster it. In fact, no such automatic process exists. To make such an assumption misses the point that it was this party that succeeded rather than another. In Scotland it could be argued that overlaying the class basis of Scottish political parties there was a nationalist dimension that merely needed expression in order for it to become a permanent feature of the political landscape. But such a view is not convincing. Firstly, while such a dimension undoubtedly did exist, it was held with quite weak intensity by most Scots: the long history of nationalist failure attests to this. Secondly, the Liberal Party, already institutionalized, presumably was capable of articulating the demand for increased Scottish autonomy. For several generations, though in a low key, it had been advocating devolution, and while the Liberal Party in both England and Scotland benefited from the prevailing disillusionment, in Scotland it was overhauled steadily by the SNP. A great deal of the credit for the success of political nationalism must be given to the SNP, who took their opportunity with energy, skill and imagination.

Even so, the SNP were fortunate in the question of timing. Quite fortuitously a happy conjunction occurred for them. By 1960, for the first time, they found themselves to be both the standard-bearers of nationalism and a united party. The collapse of MacCormick's Covenant Association left the SNP with a clear field; a number of small fringe groups existed, but they were insignificant. The history of the SNP from 1928 up to 1961 can be seen as one of 'purification', the development of a small, ideologically-united activist group. Throughout this time it had been resolving divisive party issues by sloughing off dissident elements. These issues we have already discussed. The final resolution occurred with the demise of the Covenant Association; it had been shown conclusively that the only way to power and influence was through the ballot box. Henceforth, there were no divisive strategic decisions to take; the only decisions necessary were tactical. It was, though, fortuitous that party unity and electoral disillusionment arrived at the same time. It is difficult to imagine the SNP being successful, however good the electoral opportunity, had they still been the quarrelsome and divided party of the 1930s and 1940s.

The SNP after 1961 was ideologically a continuation of the party before 1961. This, however, was not the case organizationally, for the SNP underwent a transformation that made it very different. In order to succeed electorally it was necessary for the SNP to change from being a small party of activists into a modern mass party. In politics organization is important, and the larger a party becomes the more important is organization if it is to act in a reasonably coherent manner. In a small party two-way communication between the leaders and the followers is not difficult to attain; it can largely be accomplished by means of personal contacts. With several hundred branches, though, the business of communication up and down the party hierarchy becomes very much more difficult and demands specialized attention. Similarly, when a party is small and politically insignificant it can pick and choose the topics it wishes to campaign on. But, when it grows larger and enters the political arena seriously, to some extent it has debates thrust upon it by other political contestants. It can pick its own battleground to a far lesser degree and, if it is to hold its own, a research section must be established for the collation and transmission of information to activists and candidates. Further, as the party grows it draws in new people, often with little or no political experience, and needs to train them to act effectively. And, with an increase in size, inevitably some bureaucratic machinery is needed to routinize the daily functioning of the party. Running the party becomes a business, and at least some of the leaders will become professional politicians, depending upon the party for some income. Propaganda, publicity, conferences, election deposits, agents, office rents all have to be paid for. Thus the financial basis of the party has to be developed, and all the collection of funds, subscriptions, donations, and fund-raising activities also has to be routinized. All this is implied by the change to a mass party and is necessary to ensure the permanence of the party and the coordination of its various branch units.

The rapidity with which the SNP grew between 1962 and 1968 is almost legendary. From less than two thousand members at the beginning of the decade, by 1968 there were over one hundred thousand; in 1962 there were only twenty-one branches while by 1968 there were 472. The first indication of a change in SNP fortunes occurred in the Bridgeton by-election, which was contested by Ian Macdonald, then an Ayrshire farmer. He got 18·6 per cent of the vote. This was followed in 1962 by the West Lothian by-election, the SNP candidate being William Wolfe. The SNP on this occasion got over 23 per cent of the vote, with much of the emphasis of the campaign being placed on the state of the local shale oil industry. Following the success of the Bridgeton by-election, Macdonald retired from farming to become a full-time party organizer. His Bridgeton campaign had been run very much on an *ad hoc* basis, but the excellent result persuaded Macdonald that with efficient organization the SNP had a rosy future. He aided Wolfe in his West Lothian campaign, and that result, perhaps more than any other, infused hope into the party. Arthur Donaldson, the chairman of the SNP at that time, wrote in a letter to William Wolfe:

The Executive of the National Party, having considered the excellent results already showing from the West Lothian by-election, has decided that they offer every encouragement for mounting at the next General Election the biggest campaign we have ever attempted.

Arthur Donaldson represented the older generation of nationalists. He had been active since the 1930s and had suffered to some extent for his beliefs during the war years. After West Lothian, with the expansion of the SNP, new leaders emerged. Strangely, though, none of the new leadership figures was at all charismatic. They were all sensible, level-headed individuals, but without that spark which made them stand out as exceptional figures. Many nationalist movements, past and present, have had at their head a person who characterizes the movement and who is capable of firing the enthusiasm of others. There was, though, no one of the individual stature of

MacCormick, Young, or even the whimsical Oliver Brown. Probably the first nationalist leader to attain individual prominence was Winifred Ewing, who was elected at the Hamilton by-election of 1967 to Parliament. Since 1974, though, individuals have become very much more prominent, possibly due to the greater media coverage that can be commanded by a Member of Parliament, and due to recognition of the SNP as a permanent feature of our political life.

While much of the credit for the reorganization of the SNP must go to Ian Macdonald, the SNP were fortunate to find a gifted fund raiser in Angus MacGillvray. His Alba Pools are reported to have raised over £200,000 in five years. But perhaps the most important recruit to the ranks of the SNP was William Wolfe, later to become Chairman of the Party. He was almost unknown in nationalist circles in 1962 when he stood in the West Lothian by-election, but his success there shot him up the SNP hierarchy. When he first stood in West Lothian there was not even a constituency association nor even a constitution available for one, and the policies the SNP were putting before the electorate were basically those developed in 1946–7.

Though many of the new generation of SNP leaders were newcomers to political life, many were not newcomers to public life. William Wolfe is a case in point. He was active in the scouting movement and in the Church, and had been involved for some years in the propaganda work of the Saltire Society before joining the SNP. His movement to the SNP was due to his belief that the problems of Scotland could not be solved without political change. Perhaps due to his training as a chartered accountant and to his experience in the Saltire Society, Wolfe placed a great deal of emphasis upon the value of research in the framing of public policy, a belief that has been important in the development of the party. He writes in his political autobiography:

... I am in favour of the Party examining the fabric of life in Scotland and drafting policies with a view to making proposals for improving that fabric, not only when we have self-government but also in the current political context. (*Scotland Lives*, p. 131)

He has been able to institute policy research without re-
viving the old Left versus Right factionalism within the party.
As early as 1962 the Social and Economic Inquiry Society of
Scotland was set up, and thereafter research played an important part in SNP policy formation. The SNP platform was updated annually to take account of changing economic and
political conditions. The general thrust of the SNP message was
in the same direction as that laid down in 1946–7, but much
more detailed and with practicalities more carefully considered.
Although the situation may change in the near future, owing to
the present prominence of the SNP and their probable future
activity in the proposed Scottish Assembly, the policies they
advocate (with the exception of their stand on Scottish autonomy) have not yet been clearly picked up by most of the voting
public. From the SNP point of view, it is best to see the hard
work put in on the formation of coherent policies as an investment which is liable to pay off in the future. Perhaps the only
other SNP positions which have been clearly recognized by the
electorate are the stand against the Common Market and the
demand for Scottish control of 'Scottish oil'.

Perhaps the greatest contribution of the new generation of
SNP leaders has been not so much *what* they have done, but
how they have done it. It is also important to note the sort of
people they were. The new leaders were sufficiently close to the
public image of what respectable politicians ought to be, that the
equanimity of the voting public was not disturbed. In many
ways – class, occupation and education – they are not very
different from the leadership of the established parties. In general, though, they are rather younger. The leadership style is
moderate in tone, and tends to be more pragmatic than would
normally be expected of a nationalist party. In general, the
leadership and membership are committed to persuasion and
the democratic process. This approach has not frightened the
voter in the way that a more militant and emotional appeal
might have done. With the prospect of Ulster just across the
water, a political appeal too divisive in nature would have alienated many voters. There have, however, been militant groups

within the SNP, and there are also militant groups on the fringe of the movement with militaristic ambitions. The SNP reaffirmed its belief in the democratic path to power when in 1968 membership of the 1320 Club was made incompatible with SNP membership. This question has been raised since on several occasions but the SNP position remains unchanged. The SNP, then, has benefited from the type of people who became leaders, and the style of political attack they have adopted. Because of this, in spite of the conservatism of the electorate, the switch to the SNP has not seemed too radical to the voter even though the SNP is proposing a massive change in the organization of British life.

The great success following the 1962 attempts to reorganize the party meant that by 1968 the party structure had necessarily become very much more complex. In some ways it moved closer to the model of older mass parties, although, because it was rather designed than evolved, it was more rational than the structure of the other parties. The SNP was not weighed down with historical accretion. The greater complexity of the party led to the professionalization of some leadership positions and very much more specialization of jobs. As early as 1964 a propaganda department was set up. A full-time research officer was appointed in 1968, and in that year all candidates were provided with a compendium of social and economic statistics together with their interpretation. In 1969 a Director of Communications was appointed, and a Director of Internal Training ran courses for local constituency associations in electioneering methods. Thus, between 1962 and 1970 the SNP was transformed into a modern efficient mass political party. It withstood the batterings between 1968 and 1970, and regained momentum in 1973. This extra impulse was, as we shall see, at least partly due to the strange behaviour of the Labour and Conservative Parties.

In conclusion, the rise of Scottish nationalism is difficult to relate to any general theory of political behaviour. It is something that developed out of the fabric of British life. Although the form of the demand for Scottish autonomy is new, its essence is not. The histories of England and Scotland have for many centuries been entwined, each affecting the other, sometimes decisively. This fact explains in part why there has been in Scotland such ready acceptance of the nationalist cause; it is merely the latest episode in a long sequence. The failure of other causes, the decreased attractiveness of the older parties, opened the way for the re-emergence of the ancient demand. The desire for increased autonomy has probably since the Union always been widespread in Scotland, but it has not been felt intensely and neither has it been high on the list of priorities. But it has been there, and its emergence now must indicate that there is a permanent realignment of the British political structure. While the desire has always been present and, after 1959, the opportunity for its articulation, the present power of the SNP is at least partially due to the activity of the party itself. With great skill and dedication the situation has been exploited, with the result that at present the SNP holds all the worthwhile political cards. Progressively, the established parties have lost control of the situation to the extent that at present they are not initiating policies but merely reacting politically to pressures in Scotland.

CHAPTER SEVEN

The Shaping of the Nationalist Appeal

Too often sociologists and political scientists concentrate their analysis of new political movements on social and economic conditions. This is in many ways perfectly proper, for in such an approach lies the best hope of discovering general causes of political initiatives; but, in order to understand the particular case more fully, the general data need to be supplemented by information that is more specific. It cannot be assumed that, given a particular set of socio-economic conditions, a mass political movement will develop.

The SNP could have developed as a neo-fascist movement, similar to others operating today in Britain. Or it could have followed the contemporary trend especially evident in the Third World and donned the rhetoric of socialism. Or, given the frustrations of its early history, it could have developed as an urban guerrilla movement similar to those operating a few miles away in Ulster. It chose none of these courses, but opted instead for a constitutional approach. The form of the SNP is not determined only by the social and economic characteristics of Scotland, nor even by the historical and cultural conditions in the country but also by the beliefs and visions of the nationalists themselves: how they structure their political world, what they believe is practical and feasible, and the manner in which they are viewed by the Scottish public. In order to understand nationalism in Scotland better, we must see how nationalists present themselves to the electorate, the arguments and approaches they use to persuade the electorate to support their cause, and attempt to estimate the degree of resonance their appeal strikes within the electorate.

THE HISTORICAL BACKGROUND

The success of the SNP in the 1960s meant that the vague nexus of ideas that had hitherto passed for a party programme had to be welded into a coherent and relatively consistent policy statement. Prior to 1964 the SNP could largely choose the topics upon which to campaign. However, once the party fielded large numbers of candidates at general elections, it was less easy for the candidates to frame their appeals chameleon fashion to fit particular local conditions. The SNP and other parties continue to do this quite properly in local elections, but for parliamentary elections it was necessary that the SNP begin to act in a unified fashion. Failure in this respect would have exposed them sooner or later to massive ridicule and loss of credibility.

Prior to their gains in the 1960s, SNP policies were marked by two tendencies. Firstly, the programme and the propaganda were much more negative than at present. Much of the nationalist output consisted of detailing the ills that beset Scottish society and blaming these on the activity or lack of activity of Central government. Its main bent was towards criticism rather than construction. Partially this was due to a desire among the party leadership to avoid exacerbating divisions within the party, but also because it was believed that the existence of a Scottish government would itself solve most of the problems. It was assumed that the presence of a parliament in Edinburgh was a panacea for all of Scotland's troubles, but how exactly the new government would deal with these problems was never too clear. Independence was a magic formula that made all things possible. A further reason for the construction of detailed policies is the changed future that the SNP sees for itself in an independent Scotland. Whereas in the past it regarded itself as an 'umbrella party', uniting different political interests for the achievement of a single aim, then to disperse, it now sees itself as a future government of Scotland. The SNP intends to continue as a party after independence because it believes that it has an approach to politics that is different from that of any other party in the Scottish context. Thus, although the SNP decided in principle many years ago to campaign on a comprehensive political platform, it was not until comparatively recently that the party got down to serious policy formulation.

Secondly, the development of the present nationalist programme has been characterized by a shift of emphasis away from cultural and historical matters and towards a concentration on economic, social and industrial policies. This change has occurred for a number of reasons. Partly it is due to the changing composition of the SNP, especially the leadership group. In the early days some of the most energetic and vocal figures within the leadership group were cultural notables who were not in the main interested in the mechanics of party growth or particularly knowledgeable about politics. Their interest was in the preservation of the Scottish language, concern over the anglicization of Scottish literature, the presentation and teaching of Scottish history, and their greatest fear the total loss of a distinctive Scottish culture. When the party had its early and unexpected successes, it attracted leaders of a different kind. They were concerned far more about the practical aspects of the Scottish situation. Further, with some initial success, in order to appeal to an urban industrial electorate and confirm the electoral toehold the party had gained by 1962, it was seen as necessary that the basis of the programme be broadened. The urban industrial electorate would not be greatly concerned about cultural decline when there was high unemployment, low wages, and few prospects of improved living standards.

It can also be argued that the changing status of the Scottish identity rendered excessive emphasis upon culture and history redundant. While in the past an emphasis upon the uniqueness of things Scottish was necessary to increase the awareness of regionalism as the solution to Scottish problems, today the Scottish political identity can be taken for granted and attention diverted to more practical matters. Even so, historical and cultural arguments retain an important place in Scottish nationalist propaganda, although their role is much reduced.

IDEALISM

It would be a mistake to overlook the role that idealism has played in the growth and current appeal of the SNP. While the rapid growth of the party has encouraged the incursion of some careerists who find advancement within the SNP quicker and easier than within the more rigid hierarchies of the other parties, there still remains within it a strong ethos of idealism. Because of this the party has been able to function very effectively, there always being plenty of enthusiasm at the constituency level for the more mundane tasks that are necessary to ensure electoral success. Further, this idealism has lent to SNP propaganda an evangelical quality which is perhaps the basis of its appeal to the younger voters. Compared to the other parties the SNP appears dynamic, vital and energetic, full of conviction and with hope for the future. The party offers a cause to fight for and a means of involvement in a way that the other parties do not. As yet, of course, the idealism of the SNP is untarnished by political power. It is comparatively easy to be idealistic when unencumbered either by political office or the immediate prospect of office. The test of the SNP will come when, like the Labour and Conservative Parties, it has in its propaganda to take account of political realities to a greater extent than at present.

The ideals central to the SNP are beliefs in decentralization, the rightness of economic development and local democracy, and in the existence of a distinctive and non-doctrinaire 'Scottish way' in politics. These can be seen as offshoots of the justification for greater Scottish autonomy. The principles and arguments developed by the nationalists in an English–Scottish context have been incorporated into the SNP view of a post-independence social organization of Scotland. The achievement of SNP aims is seen as being dependent upon the attainment of independence; it is not accepted that these aims can ever be implemented within a United Kingdom context. Thus, while it is true that the modern nationalist programme is very different from the vague and wordy statements of the early party, the policies of the present party can be seen as the application and extension of ideas implicit in the beliefs of the founders. In spite of very great change there remains a thread of ideological continuity, although this is not reflected in the organizational disturbances that have afflicted the movement.

As with many political programmes, while aims may be compatible in theory, in practice they often compete. So in particular situations a party may give emphasis to the attainment of one aim to the detriment of others. For example, the desire for economic growth in a modern industrial economy implies some degree of control of the economy by Government, which necessarily affects the decision-making capability of non-governmental bodies, including local government. Insofar as the SNP have faced dilemmas of this kind, they have given greater weight to economic development. It is also true, however, that because of potential oil revenues, the SNP have tended to suggest that all their aims are attainable. Clashes between ends in politics usually occur because of the scarcity of resources of one kind or another, but the SNP clearly believe that resources will be plentiful in a future independent Scotland. The imperatives of decision-making have not so far forced upon the SNP a moderation of their ambitions, but, as we shall see, there are very great problems with regard to the degree of economic freedom that is likely to be enjoyed by an independent Scottish parliament.

The central ideals of the SNP manifest themselves in a number of ways. For example, the party is opposed to the large regional councils recently set up primarily because they restrict participation and are too large to respond adequately to local community needs. The SNP therefore plan to reconstitute local authority and bring it closer to the community. At the same time it is hoped to involve the community more actively by making some of the responsibilities of the social services dependent on volunteer action. The notions of decentralization and participation also find expression in SNP industrial policy where a form of industrial democracy is envisaged. It is suggested that in addition to worker representation the controlling boards of all enterprises should have on them representatives of the community interest. Participation and organization have also been guiding principles of the organization of the SNP itself. If at times the SNP in and out of conference appears more unruly than other parties, this is because the party devolves very much more power to the branches and constituency associations than is normally the case. This may, however, be changing in practice if not in theory. In the past, when the party was smaller, contact between top and bottom was easier to maintain on an informal basis. Today there are some five hundred branches. Further, in the early days of its growth the party leadership was almost invisible, whereas now they rank with the leading politicians of other parties. This status gives them greater control of the party destiny. Also, the necessity to coordinate the activities of so large a party, and the dissemination of information, has automatically meant greater centralization.

Underlying some aspects of nationalist thought is the belief that the conditions of modern industrial society have severe effects on the individual. The industrial worker in particular, who labours within a large organization, can neither control nor find satisfaction in his work. The only control that can normally be exercised by the individual is by means of a veto, and then only collectively. The nationalist answer to alienation is to give the individual increased control through the right of active participation in both the work place and the community. This is by no means a new solution – it is not too dissimilar from what has been advocated by the Liberal Party for a number of years – but it is a solution that has attracted many adherents worldwide in contemporary times.

As with most party ideologies, there is a great deal of overlap between idealistic impulses and pragmatic considerations. For example, while participation is held to be a good in itself, in the Scottish context it is feared that the mammoth Strathclyde region would rival the Scottish parliament in the amount of resources it controlled. And, while the SNP believes in a pluralist society in general, such an accumulation of power would inhibit the ability of a Scottish government to rule effectively. A similar point can be made with regard to industrial democracy. Many people have argued recently that trade unions in the United Kingdom have too much power and that, while they may not often determine policy, they have the power to veto certain types of policy. A system of industrial democracy with shopfloor elections to the board, if it by-passes the formal union structure, can be seen as an attack on the unions. Certainly some Scottish trade unionists have interpreted SNP policy in this way, for if the function of the union is to protect the interest of the worker against management, by workers themselves playing some active part in the determination of enterprise policy, the function of the union is correspondingly lessened. Again, it may be a case of idealism and pragmatism walking hand-in-hand.

The idea that there exists a Scottish way in politics is not new by any means, but it is difficult to state clearly. It is perhaps a mood or an approach to policy-making, or a style of decision-making, rather than being a policy in itself. It is a rejection of doctrinaire automatic thinking in favour of a practical and pragmatic solution to particular problems. The genesis of such an approach is not hard to find. Firstly, there was a need to steer a course between the competing elements of left and right within the party. The idea of a Scottish way is one that could unite nationalists of different complexions. Secondly, there was a need to find a role for nationalism in a political spectrum that was dominated by parties of the conventional left, centre and right. The SNP now offers a solution that is very different from those offered by the 'English parties'. Thirdly, part of the critique of the Union is that government from Westminster is incapable, because of its remoteness, of governing in a flexible manner and taking account of varying needs in different areas. Particular problems need particular solutions which cannot be read off from a predetermined dogma. This is seen as being just as true within a future independent Scotland as at present.

Examples of the Scottish way in action we may find in the fields of housing and industrial policy. The SNP criticize Labour and Conservative Parties for the ineffectiveness of their respective housing policies, which they see as being largely caused by the desire of the other parties to achieve additional ends through their housing programme. The Labour Party have used housing policy as a means to the redistribution of wealth, as well as a way of ensuring a ready source of Labour votes, while the Conservative emphasis on owner-occupation is both an attack on Labour and a means of persuading people to vote Conservative. The real purpose of a housing policy, argue the SNP, is to increase the quality and quantity of the housing stock and other ends must be subordinated to this. Rather than approaching a situation with preconceived notions as to the right course of action, any action should be determined by what is correct and applicable in any particular situation. Similarly, the SNP argue that the whole issue of nationalization versus private enterprise has for the two largest British parties become little more than symbolic flags around which the two parties rally. If the aims of an industrial policy are to increase productivity, profitability, and perhaps redistribute power and wealth, there are many other solutions available. The stark dichotomy in policy posed by the ideologies of the major parties allows little scope for creative policy-making. The answers seem to be known in advance of the questions.

While the idea of a Scottish way in politics has many attractions, in that it would seem to allow very much greater flexibility in policy-making, such pragmatism has its dangers. In the final analysis it may not be possible to decide between different policies until there is some clear idea of the sort of society that is desired. A purely pragmatic policy process could easily degenerate into an *ad hoc* procedure designed to solve the immediate problems while not taking account of the long-term view. It is not suggested here that the SNP is at present in this position, but the danger does exist. This approach could be used to justify policies that serve only short-term ends or which are contradictory.

In general, the ideology of Scottish nationalism displays the influence of the 'small is beautiful' philosophy that has been so persuasive among radical non-Marxist groups the world over in the past decade. The philosophy is modified somewhat in that the SNP do not question the meaning or the necessity of economic development and would retain an interventionist government in an independent Scotland with strong powers. But the emphasis on de-alienation of the individual through decentralization and personal participation, the emphasis on the community, the idea of personal responsibility, and the protection of the environment are all consistent with this philosophy. By the left wing such a perspective is labelled reactionary, while the right wing view it as anachronistic.

Both charges rest, however, on value judgements. Without being able to know the future course of history, it is not possible to say what is truly reactionary or anachronistic and what is progressive. The emphasis in nationalist thinking upon decentralization and local responsibility can be seen as a throwback to economic and political theories that prevailed in the early nineteenth century; they can also be seen as a response to conditions prevailing in the late twentieth century. It may be utopian to believe that a modern industrial society can exist without high levels of government intervention, and thus substantial centralization, if only because of what individuals and groups have come to expect of government and the nature of international trade in the modern world. But even if such ideals are capable of only limited implementation, it is a form of idealism that can be powerful in motivating people politically. The truth or realism of a political doctrine is not obviously related to its propaganda value. Were this the case there would surely be far fewer political activists of all parties.

RESPONSIBILITY

While the SNP by means of its aims and ideals has generated enthusiasm among its followers, it has also increased its electoral appeal by appearing as a responsible party. The opportunity for growth was given to the nationalists by the failure of the major parties, but it was still necessary for them to exploit this opportunity. In the Scottish context this could only be done by presenting a responsible image. The SNP realized, as did the first SHRA, that Scottish political culture was very different from that of Ireland. The social cleavages were not so deep nor the bitterness so strong. There was only limited hostility towards the English. Any hint of violence would have done the nationalist cause far more harm than good, especially after the tragic developments in Ulster since 1968.

The SNP has constantly dissociated itself from the nationalist fringe groups which have either advocated or indulged in violence. Nationalists have always made a point of stressing that they would act constitutionally, although such a position, given the nature of the British constitution, still leaves wide open a number of possibilities for unconventional political activity. For example, many people would claim that a declaration of independence, or even a claim to treat for independence, following either a nationalist majority of Scottish parliamentary seats or a majority of the vote, would be unconstitutional activity in the light of the doctrine of parliamentary supremacy. Some members of the SNP would, however, consider such situations as expressing a democratic preference and thus mandating the SNP to seek independence.

The rejection of violence by the SNP leadership does not flow only from a recognition of its consequences, but also from conviction. Throughout its chequered history the SNP has always had a strong pacifist element within it derived from its early Labour Party affiliations and latterly from the CND movement. That such a rejection does flow from principle can be seen from the style of argument adopted by the SNP leadership, especially their repudiation of scapegoating methods on an ethnic basis. The state of Scottish society has been blamed on the English authorities, or the structure of authority in Britain, rather than upon the English as a nation. A distinction is maintained between the Government and English people. While arguing that Scotland is a distinctive cultural entity and ought to have control of her own destiny, the leadership have been at pains to damp down any active hostility towards the English – their attitude has rather been one of quiet derision, perhaps summarized by 'forgive them for they know not what they do'. This has been an act of positive political will, for in recent years the potential for rabble-rousing has increased with the greater salience of the Scottish identity. Some sections of the leadership have, though, inveighed against the Anglo-Scot, suggesting that Scots who do not support the cause of independence are not true Scots but have been anglicized, brainwashed, or are acting in defence of vested interests. But even this form of hostility has been in a comparatively low key.

The responsible image is heightened by other factors. The party leadership in the main tend to be very respectable figures, differing little in socio-economic status from the leadership groups in other parties. The party chairman, indeed, is a strong churchman and chartered accountant; in Scotland it is difficult to be more respectable than that. The combination of social respectability and a moderate style of argument has important consequences. The SNP are advocating large-scale changes politically, socially, and economically. Such a programme would get little support in Scotland if recommended by wild-eyed extremists. But it is very different if proposed by solid citizens who appear sensible and competent. There is very little about the SNP leadership which is likely to frighten the potential voter and much that will reassure him, for SNP leaders do not upset public expectations in their political performances.

Further, the image of the party is enhanced by the fact that it is seen as a 'clean' party, as yet untouched by corruption. Whereas the aims of politicians are frequently treated by the public with considerable scepticism, the SNP is not viewed with the same degree of cynicism. This is again partly because the party have to date achieved little power and have not been seen to either abuse their opportunities or to fail. Finally, the party spokesmen are seen by the public to be as competent and as much in command of statistics as the spokesmen of other parties. In the past in public debate, especially on television, the SNP spokesmen often appeared less informed than their political opponents. In recent years, however, the qualties of the spokesmen have improved as well as the back-up facilities open to them. The SNP leadership now appear publicly as responsible, competent, respectable and unsullied, all of which help to explain their increased appeal to the Scottish electorate.

MORALITY, JUSTIFICATION AND DESIRABILITY

The SNP in its quest for electoral success has attempted to convince the Scottish public that the claim to self-determination is justified. Without at least some degree of public conviction that greater autonomy was justified, the SNP could not hope for long-term survival. The party has also sought to demonstrate the benefits that it claims would flow from autonomy. Both arguments are bolstered by historical analysis designed to show how Scotland has been mistreated by the United Kingdom Government. While since 1962 the nationalist programme has become very much more practical, cultural and historical arguments remain pre-eminent when the right to independence is argued.

Nationalists attempt to justify their militancy by an appeal to history. Unionist and nationalist, though, will not only differ in their prescriptions for a future Scotland but will also differ radically in their interpretations of the past. Strangely, while situations in the past and present may not be clearly analogous or a causal link between the past and present very obvious, reference to a distant and possibly wholly irrelevant past can substantially affect the manner in which the present is viewed. For example, the nationalist will see the Treaty of Union as an imposition upon the Scottish nation by a corrupt and self-seeking, unrepresentative minority, while the unionist will see it as an act of wise and far-sighted statesmanship in the face of popular clamour. Similarly, with respect to the regional policies of central government over the past forty years, the nationalist will see them as inhibiting the growth of indigenous industry and aiding the economic colonization of Scotland, while the unionist will claim that they have always been necessary to ameliorate the worst effects of the Scottish economic decline. In support of political positions history is infinitely flexible.

The aim of all ideologies is to attempt to weld disparate and untidy realities into a coherent perspective which contains within it prescriptions for future political action. The ideology of Scottish nationalism is no different. It aims to tie the past to the present in such a way as to make it appear that Scotland has forever been struggling against English domination, in spite of the fact that during the 270 years of the Union nationalist expression has been very sporadic and muted for most of the time. Further, modern nationalists attempt to present themselves as the legitimate carriers of this historical struggle. Wallace and Bruce, ancient heroes of Scotland, are lauded as ancestors of the contemporary movement and celebrated annually with great ceremony. In proposing their view of history, the nationalists have very great propaganda advantages over the unionists. Firstly in contrast to the unionist view of history, their version is simple, straightforward, and easily understood. It has the virtue of seeming to explain a great deal in the Scottish situation. Secondly, the nationalist version is able to mobilize values dear to Scots in a way that is not easily open to the unionist. The unionist cannot and probably would not wish to deny the greatness of Wallace and Bruce, but he cannot utilize the folk images of the early patriots to support his case. The nationalist, though, can seek to convert the high regard with which these and other cultural figures are popularly viewed into support for the nationalist cause. And, should the nationalist view of history be accepted, such a conversion is not a big step for the individual to take.

The historical perspective encouraged by the SNP claims that Scots have interests which are different from those of the United Kingdom, and that these interests have consistently been subordinated to English interests, with the result that Scotland has become economically backward in a European context. The UK Government has acted, either through malignity, neglect or incompetence, to exploit Scotland and deny her the means of advancement. While, on the one hand, the SNP – unwittingly aided by the media – have by their emphasis on things Scottish been increasing the importance of Scottishness to the individual, they are also claiming that Scotland is being denied that which is rightfully hers by an unsympathetic government. Scots have always felt that they are unique within the United Kingdom, but have not always claimed on this basis the right to preferential or even different treatment by central government. But the nationalist view of history encourages the belief that Scotland has been ill-treated and increases the desire of Scots to benefit disproportionately from the newly-discovered wealth off Scotland's coasts. From the nationalist point of view the exploitation of North Sea oil by the United Kingdom rather than Scotland becomes one more example of the economic rape of Scotland.

Having established that Scotland on the basis of her cultural and historical peculiarities has interests which are different from the rest of the United Kingdom, nationalists then suggest that Scotland can achieve statehood and full national expression through the ballot box. In most societies the territorial integrity of the state is unquestioned; it is accepted as part of the natural order of things. The nationalists, by their emphasis on Scotland's status in the past and the possibility of change in the future, call into question the continuity of the United Kingdom. This is posed to the Scottish people as a matter of choice, something they can decide by flexing their political muscles. Once the continuity of the United Kingdom is seen as a matter of choice, whether that existence is deemed worthwhile becomes a matter for open assessment. Where no choice was perceived imperfect social conditions were passively accepted; once choice is perceived as possible then those same conditions become grounds for indignation. Demands are placed on Central Government which cannot immediately be met, but the electorate is offered a vision of a future Scotland within which these demands will be satisfied.

The SNP, like all radical parties, seek to change political perspectives. Thus the party argues from history and culture to the status of being Scottish and the right of self-determination. But these justifications for the claim to independence are supplemented by the nationalist version of what the future independent Scotland would look like. Scottish eyes are directed to the South East of England, to Norway or Finland, to see what the future could be like. Improvements in housing, welfare, health care, pensions, wages or the environment are all promised, to be funded from the revenues of North Sea oil. The SNP have over the past decade launched a multi-pronged attack on the loyalties of Scottish people, giving them a cause to fight for, a new place and status in the world, and a hope for the future. At present the party seems to be triumphantly succeeding on all fronts.

Unionists have responded, if tardily, to the nationalist challenge. While the SNP has been justifying its demands for independence, the unionists have been giving reasons why the Scottish people must, or are obliged to, remain within the United Kingdom. The essence of the unionist moral case is that the nationalist demand for independence is cynical opportunism with regard to North Sea oil, especially bearing in mind the manner in which the rest of the United Kingdom has been supporting a failing Scottish economy for many years. After many years of support, Scotland owes the UK a great deal. Further, it is unthinkable that had oil been discovered off the coast of Hampshire or Suffolk that Scotland would not have benefited as much as any English region. There would have been no talk of England shedding the less profitable parts of the United Kingdom in order to enjoy the proceeds of oil alone. As it is, 'English' natural gas is flowing into Glaswegian homes and this has hardly been mentioned. From the unionist perspective, it is the duty of Scotland to aid the rest of the United Kingdom in this time of need.

The SNP reject the charge of economic opportunism. The nationalists state, and quite correctly, that their position on independence was established long before the presence of oil was even suspected. Further, the link between nationalist success at the polls and the discovery of oil is seen as merely fortuitous. It is pointed out that the SNP were on the march electorally long before 1974 when they made their major breakthrough. The 1974 election is seen as the continuance of a trend that began as far back as 1962. Although it is difficult to believe that the oil issue had nothing to do with nationalist success, it is clear that nationalism was not caused by oil. As we shall see, oil had the effect of making SNP policies appear feasible, thus allowing the emergence and expression of a suppressed popular bias for greater autonomy. Oil reduced the cost, both psychological and material, of being nationalist.

FEASIBILITY

The SNP may convince the Scottish public that its leaders are responsible individuals. It may stimulate a high degree of enthusiasm among a minority, and persuade a majority that greater autonomy is desirable. But unless the party is able to convince the electorate, or at least the opinion-leaders within the public, that its proposals are feasible, its success will be limited. At best it can only operate as a vehicle of protest and its existence will be ephemeral, dependent upon the extent to which the Scottish public perceive it as a means for putting pressure on government.

In the previous chapter we noted the manner in which the SNP achieved political credibility. This was also dependent upon public perception; SNP policies had to be seen as sensible and capable of implementation. Throughout the ages political thinkers have constructed utopias which have had little persuasive power because of their extreme implausibility. There is considerable evidence that for many years the aims of nationalism had a sympathetic hearing from the Scottish public, but clearly this sympathy was not translated into votes. It is therefore reasonable to suppose that when the nationalists were culturally orientated and internally fragmented, with ill-defined and often inconsistent policies, the public did not perceive their cause as a feasible political alternative.

Feasibility, though, does not depend upon the SNP alone. It is related to the political offerings of the other parties in electoral competitions. What appears to the voter as feasible and capable of implementation will depend upon the alternatives, the ability of other parties to attack the economic basis of the nationalist case, and their ability to communicate with the public. Recently devolution has become the single most important issue in British politics. A great deal of the debate will be about the economics of devolution, and the onus is now upon the unionist to state his case. In the propaganda race nationalists have got a head start, and only now are unionists beginning to organize their arguments coherently. However, given the quality of their previous responses, it must be considered an open question as to whether the unionist parties in Scotland have either the political will or the propagandist ability to meet the nationalist case.

While the SNP remained a fringe party the major parties hardly bothered to meet their economic case; the nationalists were either ignored or ridiculed. With the growth of the SNP the major attack upon them was in terms of the practicality of their case. It was argued that Scotland was subsidized by England and was heavily dependent on English markets and capital, and thus independence was not economically feasible. A number of academics studied the economic relationship between England and Scotland. A major problem with such studies was that important gaps existed in the economic statistics available, since not all such data are gathered on a regional basis. In terms of government revenue and expenditure it appeared that Scotland was subsidized, and in general academic opinion concurred with this view. However, the corollary of this was rejected, and no credibility was given to the view that Scotland was too poor to be independent. If so many Third World countries could claim the right to self-determination when they had trouble in even feeding their populations, it was nonsense to argue that Scotland could not be independent. The real questions were whether the standard of living would fall with self-government and whether the independence of Scotland would be more than nominal, so dominated was she by the size of her southern neighbour.

There were several nationalist responses to the suggestion that Scotland is subsidized. One response was to deny it completely, or even to suggest that Scotland subsidized England. In this form of argument the more intangible economic factors were stressed, such as the brain-drain to England. Because of the gaps in the data it was possible to argue this case, albeit unconvincingly. Another response, this from cultural nationalists, was to deny that economics had anything to do with nationalism. Nationalism is about the preservation and enhancement of the Scottish spirit as reflected in art and artifacts. Political independence is a necessary condition for the progress of art, to prevent the gradual anglicization of Scottish culture. Independence was not a bread-and-butter economic issue, and certainly not a bargainable commodity.

The most frequent response, however, was to recognize the fact of English subsidization and still maintain that the economic case for independence was credible. On occasions it was even accepted that for a short while after independence the standard of living might fall. This was seen as a cost that would have to be borne if the reconstruction of Scotland was to be achieved. The basis of this argument was that Scotland needed to be subsidized because of the present and historic policies of Central Government and, so long as the union with England was maintained, improvement in the Scottish situation was not possible. Scottish problems could only be solved in the context of an independent Scotland. Behind this view lay a strong belief in the capacities and energies of the Scottish people, which in the centralized state of the United Kingdom were not being utilized. A Scottish parliament close to the Scottish people would supply the conditions within which Scots could act to further Scottish ends. The people would therefore not be constrained and inhibited by government policies designed for English problems but inappropriate to Scottish circumstances.

Those who rejected this form of analysis, or who doubted the ability of the Scottish economy to reconstitute itself within the foreseeable future, and so stressed the necessity of the English tie, were derided for their 'begging bowl' mentality. It is perhaps fair to say that by the late 1960s nationalists were getting the better of public debate on the economy, partly by default and partly through their greater skill in propaganda, but their arguments had not impressed expert opinion overmuch.

The discovery and subsequent exploitation of oil radically changed the whole situation. Whereas nationalists prior to this discovery were struggling to convince the Scottish public of the practicality of their proposals, their case was all of a sudden much more persuasive. Estimates of how much oil there is and what percentage of it is commercially exploitable vary a great deal, but it is undeniable that vast revenues will accrue to the government controlling the resource. The SNP claim it for Scotland. Many Scots do not support the SNP. Even more are not in favour of complete independence. But few now doubt the economic feasibility of the ambitious plans the SNP have for the development of an independent Scotland.

The SNP are far from unwilling to use the North Sea bonanza for propaganda purposes. In one campaign they posed the question 'Rich Scots or Poor Britons?' While the presence of oil lies behind most of their policies, in the past grandiose plans in many fields were suspect because of the lack of any obvious means to fund them. Now the means are at hand. All can be paid for from the North Sea oil revenues once Scotland is free. Oil in the context of independence is the universal panacea for all of Scotland's problems. Its discovery washed away the doubts of many voters and increased confidence and optimism among nationalists. There are now relatively few constraints on the expression of nationalist utopianism.

The discovery of oil galvanized the political situation in Scotland in a number of ways. Because oil was seen as being vital to the British economic recovery, and because its presence also seemed to increase the possibility of a successful independence movement, the interests and needs of Scots assumed an importance in the political arena that hitherto they had not possessed. Discussion about devolution had begun seriously in 1968, but was rather designed to delay matters until the Scottish protest had withered away, as had previous nationalist surges. When the material and psychological effects, not least in the world money markets, were seen to be potentially catastrophic should the SNP succeed in detaching Scotland from the United Kingdom, things took on a new significance. The political leaders of all parties had been stressing the importance of oil in the British economic recovery, and the internal effects of its loss could not be calculated.

One of the more lurid prophecies was that a crisis would arise in Britain as severe as that which overtook the ill-fated Weimar Republic in Germany. Scots, recognizing the dependency of the United Kingdom upon Scottish resources, became more assertive while government hastened to mollify them, fearful of the consequences of failure. The stakes of the game had increased dramatically. Further, because of the newly perceived dependency upon Scotland, the reverse of what Scots were used to, the status of being Scots increased. They were a force to be reckoned with and took pride in the fact. Another important consequence was that nationalists were no longer looked upon as impractical dreamers, but were seen rather as being hard-headed and realistic in the field of economics.

One of the most beneficial results to come out of the political furore has been that those in favour of retaining the United Kingdom have been forced to present their case more coherently than in the past, as well as to develop a reasoned critique of the nationalist case. One of the spin-offs from the debate may well be a searching examination of the system of government in the United Kingdom as a whole. Nationalists, rather patronizingly, do in fact suggest that their presence in the UK political system will have beneficial effects for the English. They believe that they are providing new solutions to old problems that are as prevalent in England as in Scotland; the political argument will shake the English out of their staid complacency and force them to put their own house in order.

Many of the unionist arguments used in reply were moralistic in tone, intent on reminding Scots of their debts and obligations. Few people enjoy being reminded of these, and such an approach was unlikely to be successful by itself. More recently, however, the unionists have attacked the nationalist argument on a number of other grounds. Broadly, they argue that the nationalists have got their economics wholly wrong or at best have not understood the implications that such vast revenues would have on the Scottish economy; that the nationalists are making unwarranted assumptions about the nature of the English reaction; and that as yet there are unanswered questions about the ownership of offshore mineral rights. It is also suggested that the SNP is misleading the public in a number of ways.

One of the primary arguments used by unionists is that if Scotland did gain independence and control of the oil revenues one immediate effect would be a revaluation of the Scottish currency against all other major currencies, including sterling. This would mean that Scottish exports would become more expensive. Since many Scottish industries are remaining competitive at present only with difficulty, in spite of constant devaluation, the level of unemployment in Scotland would increase a great deal. Nationalists, of course, reject this view. They point to other small nations with large resources (usually Norway) which have not suffered the dire consequences predicted. Further, they suggest that whereas unionists were a few years ago dismissing the nationalist economic argument on the basis that Scotland was too poor to be independent, the argument now seems to be that Scotland is too rich. However, unionists point out that a major difference between the Norwegian and Scottish cases would be the speed at which transition to an oil-rich nation occurred. The Norwegians had a number of years to prepare. The unionists also argue that SNP policies would lead to an increase in the rate of inflation. They maintain that it would not be possible to pump so much money into the Scottish economy in so short a time, in an attempt to regenerate Scottish industry, without incurring an inflationary upswing. In addition, in order to fulfil their election pledges, for example with regard to wages, pensions, housing and the social services, the future Scottish government (which is assumed to be an SNP administration) would be forced to finance a consumer-orientated boom which again would have inflationary effects.

These arguments are rejected on three grounds. Firstly, a Scottish government would slow down the rate of oil extraction, both to accord with the needs of Scotland and to conserve the resource. The unionist criticism rests on the assumption that Scotland would continue to extract oil in line with the targets set by the United Kingdom government. Secondly, it is suggested that not all of the oil revenues have to be invested in Scotland. They can be given in foreign aid, invested abroad, or even loaned to England to help her over her current economic crisis. Finally, it is believed by the SNP that they have sufficient rapport with the Scottish people to have accepted a policy of gradual increase in living standards. Unionists would deny that the rate of extraction can be slowed down, at least initially, for there would be huge compensation to be paid to the British government for their investment, as well as a clash with the oil companies. An SNP government would need such money desperately.

It is further argued by unionists that the whole SNP case rests on the belief that a British government would negotiate with the nationalists in a gentlemanly fashion if the SNP got a majority of votes or seats and decided to seek independence. It should not be assumed that a British government would act in such a complacent manner. The spectre of military action in Scotland would be unlikely – although such a reaction has been envisaged by some – but retaliatory economic action is quite possible. Scotland would be suing for status as an independent foreign country and could be treated as such, although the SNP claim that a close economic tie with no import duties or customs barrier would be their aim. Between 40 and 60 per cent of Scottish exports go to England; if the Westminster government decided to place a tariff on these goods they would be very uncompetitive with similar English goods. Further, it cannot be expected that a future British government would continue to place orders in Scotland, and neither would a Scottish administration with its smaller needs be able to take over this function. According to one estimate, this would involve the loss of some fifty thousand jobs. In addition, the Scottish level of unemployment is only kept as low as it is by massive emigration, sometimes as many as forty thousand a year leaving

Scotland. Around one half of these go to England for work. With England in recession, it cannot be expected that an influx of migrant workers on such a scale would be acceptable, since these workers in terms of skills and ability would be directly in competition with native workers.

The SNP do not accept this argument. In their view England needs Scotland just as badly as Scotland needs England. For example, access to Scottish oil would give England security of supply and possibly preferential terms. Further, according to the nationalist analysis, England would have strong pressure put on her by both NATO and her EEC partners to reach a peaceable understanding with Scotland. The SNP believe that Scotland, because of her strategic geographical position with coasts exposed to both the North Sea and the Atlantic, is vital to the NATO defence system; while the EEC would need Scotland within the market to take advantage of her resources and to be some assurance against further OPEC pressure. There would be the same conditions between England and Scotland as exist between member countries of the EEC. In general, nationalists believe that independence could be negotiated harmoniously and that a British government would be constrained from taking any retaliatory action. They do not see the position as being similar to the period preceding the Union of 1707, when the economic pressure from England affected Scotland seriously. It is necessary for the nationalists, if they are to retain the support of their less committed followers, that the secession be presented as being reasonably cost-free. Should the process of gaining independence and the immediate economic consequences become generally perceived as being deleterious to Scotland's interests, some SNP support could fade away. In reality, it is unlikely that, if secession should occur it would be particularly harmonious. While government may be prepared to act in an accommodating fashion, English public opinion would be very hostile. There are too many hopes pinned on North Sea oil, some of them unrealistic, but giving some hope of a better future amid the current economic gloom.

Unionists also charge nationalists with misleading the Scottish public with respect to the rate at which a reconstitution of Scottish industry could be achieved. Any such plans must be considered as being very long-term, ten years probably being an absolute minimum. Such a regeneration does not depend upon investment level alone, but is also strongly affected by the availability of a research and development capacity, managerial expertise and an appropriately skilled labour force. Research and development capability can to some extent be bought, but retraining is an expensive and lengthy process. It will often depend upon the training of new workers rather than the conversion of older workers reluctant to abandon long-used skills. The nationalists have been accused of being vague about the actual process of regeneration and what it would cost the worker. They sometimes give the impression that a new and buoyant Scottish economy would emerge shortly after independence. In response to this form of attack nationalists go back to the argument they put forward in the pre-oil era; regeneration is the result of hard work, enthusiasm and the appropriate non-constrictive political and economic environment. It is finally a question of having faith in the Scottish people.

'It's Scotland's Oil' is a slogan that has proved to have considerable public appeal. But how would such a claim stand up in international law? At present the question of the exploitation of the sea bed is a matter of international debate, but in the British context certain general points can be made. Currently the sea demarcation line between England and Scotland flows from the coastal border point parallel to the lines of latitude. If this practice were followed post-independence, virtually all the oil fields (but not the gas) would fall within the Scottish sector. The demarcation has in the past been necessary because of the differences in English and Scottish law. It is unlikely, however, that during negotiations for independence this practice would be followed. Rather, the demarcation line would probably be drawn at right angles to the 'coastal trend' at the coastal border point which would send it east-north-east into the North Sea. Such a line would probably bisect the Montrose oil field and place Lomond, Josephine, Auk and Argyll within the English sector rather than the Scottish.

But the problem does not end there, for nationalists are assuming that an independent Scotland would include the Orkney and Shetland Isles, both of which consider themselves to be culturally very different from the Scottish mainland. Nationalists argue that since both communities are too small to be admitted to the United Nations, they cannot be considered to have the right to independent statehood. It has been suggested that the Isles have a similar status within a future Scotland as that enjoyed by the Isle of Man at present in Britain, although in passing it might just be noted that there is a considerable body of opinion on the Isle of Man in favour of breaking the close tie with the United Kingdom. In the Orkneys and Shetlands many islanders are dubious of the value of Edinburgh control. The general point is, though, that if the Orkney and Shetland Isles successfully claimed independence, or if they retained their connection with the United Kingdom while Scotland secedes, Scotland's rights to North Sea oil would be reduced by about two-thirds of those fields at present considered commercially exploitable.

While there is little doubt in the public mind at present about the economic feasibility of the SNP proposals, it is very desirable that before any irreversible steps are taken the nationalist economic case should be examined more carefully. Economists are a contentious group, and it is unlikely that any consensus on the economic prospects of an independent Scotland would emerge from their ranks. In general, they are not noted for accurate forecasting even in stable political conditions. However, in spite of the confusion and uncertainty that undoubtedly would surround such a debate it is important that such vital matters be publicly aired. Scotland in particular, and possibly the United Kingdom as a whole, could only benefit from a healthy public discussion.

PUBLIC AWARENESS OF SNP POLICIES

The SNP have devoted a great deal of time and energy to policy formulation, but it is clear that, apart from a few major issues, the larger nationalist programme has not got through to the Scottish public in force. This lack of a wider public appreciation should not particularly surprise us, for surveys conducted in liberal democracies over the past forty years have demonstrated consistently that voters seldom have detailed information about policies. Party programmes are complex documents, and many of the policies they contain are not seen by the voter to be relevant to his circumstances. Instead, the voter is often aware of the general direction or tendency of a party, and has a perception of its effectiveness upon which his decision will be made.

The lack of a detailed awareness of nationalist policies is increased by the difficulty of placing the SNP on the conventional political spectrum. Not only do the SNP reject the traditional dichotomy of left and right, but their political opponents label them in different ways. The Conservative Party has in the past inveighed against their dangerous radical tendencies, while the Labour Party has referred to them as 'Tartan Tories'. Information in politics, as in any other field, is best retained where there is a clear organizing principle, but in the case of the SNP this is not readily apparent even to sophisticated voters. A minority opinion within the SNP has described the party as social democratic in an attempt to get some placement on the spectrum, but this view does not appear to be particularly influential within the party.

We should be careful, however, not to dismiss the SNP programme as a mish-mash of policies chosen only for their electoral appeal. It was suggested earlier that there are clear principles behind nationalist policies, but that these do not fit readily into a left-right framework. It should be remembered also that what passes for consistency in the programmes of other parties is more often the result of our having grown accustomed to expect certain types of policy to be bundled together rather than to any natural or logical unity among the policies themselves. In a few years' time, perhaps, we may more readily accept the bundle proposed by the SNP.

In their attacks on the SNP the major UK parties tend to concentrate on the independence issue while ignoring other aspects of the nationalist programme. From the point of view of the major parties this approach makes good sense, firstly because most SNP policies are framed in the light of an independent Scotland, and secondly because such a concentration does not draw further invidious attention to the socio-economic problems of Scotland. Further, public awareness of party solutions has probably been inhibited by the characteristics of the Scottish political system, although these have undoubtedly been changing rapidly under the influence of SNP methods of propaganda. Scotland is a much smaller country than England, with a very much more personalized political system, dominated by Glasgow and Edinburgh. In addition, activists of different parties are very much more likely to know each other. Hence political statements have tended to be directed towards political activists of other parties rather than towards the general public. The level of political discussion has often been high, but also often incomprehensible to the less politicized section of the electorate.

It is extremely probable that the level of public awareness to SNP policies will rise sharply in the near future as a consequence of the changing political situation in Britain. Whether excluded from control of a regional assembly or not, the SNP have a platform far more potent than their presence at Westminster can ever be from which to attack both Central Government and the major UK parties in Scotland. The SNP will be putting forward solutions to Scottish problems which will be incompatible with Central Government objectives. Intense political conflict can therefore be expected both between the parties in Scotland and between Scottish interests and Westminster. The greater the intensity of the debate, and the more vital the matters at stake, the more informed will the electorate become of the issues involved. Given the present circumstances, it is inconceivable that the political temperature in Scotland will not rise sharply.

CHAPTER EIGHT

The Future of Nationalism in Scotland

The story of nationalism in Scotland will not end with the passing of the Scotland Bill. It is conceivable that in the not too distant future Scotland could again become an independent state. The march to independence is not, however, inevitable, as some commentators have assumed. There is no historical law that maintains that social groups with a strong sense of ethnic identity have to express this through statehood. There are numerous examples of self-conscious ethnic minorities living peacefully within larger political units. There are, however, many cases where ethnic differences have led to terrible violence and bloodshed, sometimes full-scale civil war, and even attempted genocide. While none of these extremes appears to be likely in the Scottish context, it is probable that the future relationship between Scotland and England will be unstable for some time to come. That this is likely to be the case is due to the long history of political mismanagement of the devolution issue by Parliaments that has continued until the present day.

It should be pointed out, however, that mismanagement has not occurred through either the stupidity or the malignity of legislators at Westminster. Such an explanation is too simple and does not do justice either to the calibre of the legislators or to the historical context of nationalism. In Chapter Six it was pointed out that nationalism was given its initial opportunity by the ideological convergence of the two major parties. The emergence of consensus politics, the era of 'Butskellism', lowered the political temperature and the ability of the Labour and Conservative Parties to mobilize the faithful. Since then, however, the responses of the major parties to nationalism have been inadequate and have had the effect of encouraging the growth of political nationalism in Scotland.

Three factors have determined the responses of the major parties. Firstly, the nature of modern Scottish nationalism was misperceived and this seriously affected the quality of the political response. Secondly, the type of question most proper to a consideration of the devolution issue has taken second place to electoral pragmatism, with the effect that the political response has been marked more by expediency than wisdom. Thirdly, nationalism and its implications have been ill-considered because the issue has been thought by many legislators to be irrelevant to the problems facing the United Kingdom.

The major parties perceived Scottish nationalism in a manner conditioned by its past performance. Throughout the twentieth century, roughly every ten years or so, there have been small nationalist surges culminating in the Covenant movement of the early 1950s. Even that spectacular attempt to force devolution into the political arena failed. Each time noise and rhetoric had been generated only for the political wing of the nationalist movement to collapse, leaving no permanent mark on the political system. A few votes here or there, even a parliamentary seat in unusual wartime circumstances, did not persuade the major parties of the seriousness of the demand for devolution. Hence, nationalism in the 1960s came to be classed with previous politically insignificant surges. Earlier experience suggested the appropriate response; inactivity and non-response with a dash of deference to Scottish national pride on the campaign platform.

The fact that the organization of contemporary nationalism in Scotland was very different from its earlier manifestations went largely unnoticed. Also, the situation of the SNP with respect to rival nationalist organizations was different, as was the political context within which it was acting. The steady incremental growth of an electorally orientated movement and the increasing grasp by the leadership of the realities of modern mass politics were ignored. The growth of grass-roots support, often in the context of local rather than national politics, and the development of a competent leadership cadre had no impact on the quality of the response the SNP stimulated. Response, if it occurred at all, was by individuals rather than parties, and

lacking any constraining party-line tended to be somewhat idio-
syncratic. It was not until 1967 that it was recognized that the
nationalists could be inconvenient. Even then, attention was
directed at stalling the issue and rhetorically stealing the
nationalists' clothes rather than considering the issues themselves. In the minds of many political analysts the 1970 General
Election confirmed expectations of the imminent collapse of the
nationalist vote. It was a classic case of seeing a situation and
interpreting it in the light of preconceptions.

Had the major parties in 1968 maintained their previous consensus, and had they both set their faces firmly against any form
of devolution, they might have weathered the approaching
storm. The anti-devolution case could have been constructively
argued. This was before North Sea oil became a political factor
and the unionist economic argument had much to commend it.
It is perhaps instructive to look at the case of Tam Dalyell,
who has since 1962 rebuffed the electoral challenge from SNP
Chairman William Wolfe at West Lothian by remaining totally
opposed to any form of legislative devolution. The flood-gates
burst in 1968, however, and the voter was presented with a
variety of devolutionary schemes and anti-devolutionary pro-
nouncements that showed the major parties to be very confused
about the issue. Devolution became an issue almost overnight
and it seemed at one time as if the Labour and Conservative
Parties were prepared to outbid each other for the Scottish vote
in an attempt to dish the nationalists, without, however, any
real desire to bring about legislation. Only the SNP gained from
such a situation. The political battles both within and between
the major parties, while mild compared to the post-1974
struggles, only served to aid the SNP. They gained credibility
in the public mind. A vote for the SNP meant that London would
take notice of Scotland. The SNP were effective in getting
things moving. Any meaningful evaluation of the devolution
issue was, though, deferred by shunting the issue off to a Royal
Commission on the Constitution by the Labour Government,
and later to a party committee by the Conservative opposition.

The aim was to take the issue out of the political present and to wait for the cause of the furore to fade away.

After 1970, nationalism in Scotland was popularly considered a spent force. Perhaps one sign of the loss of interest in the issue by the major parties was the massive re-organization of local government that took place before the Royal Commission on the Constitution reported. Had devolution been seriously considered as a constitutional possibility, this very expensive and highly disruptive re-organization would surely have been deferred. With the very real possibility of a Scottish Assembly now in front of us, much of the re-organization will prove redundant. The demise of the SNP was, however, very much exaggerated, as the results of the February and October 1974 General Elections showed conclusively. The strategy of deferment and delay accompanied by the appropriate rhetoric had speedily to be revised. Strangely, after so many years of discussion, including a Royal Commission, neither major party had managed to formulate a coherent policy. Both parties remained split on the issue, the Labour Party to the extent that a small breakaway party emerged from its ranks.

Hence, the expectation of the collapse of nationalism (and even the belief that it had collapsed), derived from the past performance of nationalism, meant that no serious policy formulation took place. Devolution was not granted the status of a genuine issue by the decision-makers. The resulting confusion that occurred, when nationalism was seen as a force threatening the vital interests of the major parties, led to the Scottish electorate being wooed as never before. The periphery became important. This only served to affirm the worth of the SNP in the eyes of the voter, an effect that was enhanced when the potentialities of North Sea oil became known.

The second factor that prevented effective response to the devolution issue by the major parties was that they were more interested in the electoral consequences of nationalism rather than the issue itself. Many Scots, even firm Labour and Conservative voters, have ever been resentful of the long arm of

Westminster and really did desire more regional autonomy. There is some evidence that this is a long-standing desire; certainly the 1932 Beaverbrook Poll, while not rigorously conducted, would seem to confirm this. The major parties, though, considered the issue mainly in the light of what they had to do in order not to lose any more votes. The response was grudging and reluctant. It was based on tactical expediency rather than any desire to reach the root of the problem. As they were based on tactical electoral considerations rather than conviction, the policies of both parties wavered in the wind without consistency or stability. The Conservative Party eventually, after much discussion and front-bench resignations, tended towards the advocacy of a Scottish talking chamber with little effective power, while the Labour Party, with more to lose in terms of votes and parliamentary seats, felt forced to give more substance to the appearance. However, while legislation for devolution now looks likely to succeed, the basic reluctance of Parliament has affected the type of legislation put forward. Rather than solving any problems, instead it creates a host of new problems for future governments.

The third factor influencing the inadequacy of the response was that, given the nature of the problems facing the United Kingdom in this crucial period, questions of regional autonomy and devolution seemed wholly irrelevant. The United Kingdom for nearly twenty years has been lurching from one crisis to another, culminating in three-day weeks, frightening inflation, and unacceptable levels of unemployment. The spectres of the Great Depression and the consequences of hyper-inflation in pre-war Germany were before legislators. The answers to the economic, social, and industrial problems facing the United Kingdom were to be sought in tighter government control of the economy – the control of the growth of money supply, cutbacks in projected public spending, control of increases in wages and salaries, and a host of additional measures. Nationalism in this context was intrusive and divisive and had no clear relationship to the solution of the problems facing the United Kingdom. Indeed, it was argued that genuine devolution, where a legislature had some fiscal control with some revenue-raising powers, could interfere with central government economic strategy. It was inconceivable that an assembly north of the border could be allowed to jeopardize the recuperative economic measures being enacted. Effective legislative devolution was, therefore, out from the start. Again, many English members had little understanding of the importance of devolution to many Scots. In the main they interacted with Scots who were wedded to the United Kingdom political structure, with the result that the passions attending the issue were only dimly perceived. To many Scots, however, the question of effective devolution was intimately linked and very relevant to the socio-economic problems of Scotland. As early as 1825 the view had been expressed that measures appropriate to the English economic situation were not always appropriate to Scotland, and it was felt that with a measure of autonomy Scots could aid themselves more effectively than by relying on the benefits flowing from central control. Due to their perception of what were the important political questions, many English legislators consigned the nationalists to the crackpot category, a lunatic fringe to be kept quiet while the really important issues were dealt with. But, in a democracy, if a sufficient number of people think something is important, it becomes important, however irrelevant their leaders may consider it.

This background has conditioned the type of legislation put before Parliament. Lacking any clear consensus within either party, and with electoral considerations weighing heavily, the legislation attempts to satisfy a variety of opinions, as well as placating Scottish electoral opinion. The current legislation is an exercise in coalition building, being nicely judged to enable a parliamentary majority to be found for it. The first devolution measure, the Scotland and Wales Bill, was a disaster, not least in that it linked Scotland and Wales together when the circumstances of the two countries are so very different. This error is avoided in the later proposals. The first devolution legislation failed in March 1977, ostensibly because of the failure of the Government to impose a guillotine on debate. In reality the bill succeeded only in uniting in strange alliance all those opposed to it, whether this was because it devolved too many powers or too few powers. The bill failed because it satisfied no one. It is arguably the case that the second devolution measure, the Scotland Bill, does not satisfy many legislators either. However, the continuing strength of the SNP as reflected in the opinion polls, plus the prospect of an approaching General Election, have focused the parliamentary mind wonderfully. The Government has won the crucial guillotine vote, and in the Scottish case it is most unlikely that the proposed referendum will overturn the legislation.

The second devolution bill, the Scotland Bill, is an improvement on the earlier version. The proposed Assembly now has the power to dissolve itself in cases of stalemate. Further, the heavy hand of the Scottish Secretary of State is somewhat lightened. In cases of dispute as to whether a matter falls within the 'legislative competence' of the Assembly, the problem is to be referred to the Judicial Committee of the Privy Council. The grant to the new Assembly is to be assessed every four years rather than annually. This will aid forward planning. More importantly, it will lessen conflict in that the amount of bargaining will be reduced between the central and regional legislatures, and the disproportionate share of government resources going to Scotland will be less obvious to the less prosperous English regions.

While these changes are to be welcomed, they must be recognized as being purely cosmetic. They do nothing to remove the inherent weakness that was apparent in the earlier bill. In 1968 such a measure may have been successful in buying off the Scots, but in 1978 it is inadequate. If the drive towards an independent Scotland is to be halted, only two positions are feasible – either no devolution at all by choice rather than prevarication and indecision, or full-scale federalism. All intervening positions, of which the new Assembly is an example, will be unstable in that they provide ample opportunities for the exacerbation of conflict by a regional Assembly so inclined. The structure of the proposed relationship between Westminster and Calton Hill allows every chance for the SNP to 'scapegoat' the Westminster Parliament.

The proposed Scottish Assembly has no power to raise monies; it is wholly dependent upon Westminster for its revenues. Yet it is responsible for spending money granted to it. The Assembly will only work if there is some ideological accord between the Scottish and Parliamentary administrations, for any Scottish executive has to accept that its freedom of action is severely curtailed by the Scotland Bill. For example, the Secretary of State may reject a bill if he believes it to be incompatible with the obligations imposed on the United Kingdom by virtue of our membership of the EEC. This includes an ever-widening field of social, industrial, and agricultural legislation. More importantly, the Secretary of State has the right to recommend to Parliament that an enactment of the Assembly should be rejected if it 'indirectly' affects matters reserved to Parliament or is deemed to be not in the 'public interest'. Hence, in spite of the introduction of the Judicial Committee of the Privy Council to soften the interface between the Scottish Assembly and the Secretary of State, means exist whereby the wishes of the Scottish Assembly can be overridden even while ostensibly acting within their legislative competence. Further, the Scotland Bill proposes strong constraints on the way in which the grant can be used. For example, the ability of Scottish executives to initiate policies for industrial development and the reduction of unemployment will be severely circumscribed in that their policies must follow 'guidelines' laid down by the Secretary of State with the approval of the Treasury.

The list of constraints upon the Assembly's freedom of decision-making could be considerably lengthened. Clearly, the powers of a legislature to spend monies it has not raised must be severely circumscribed; to spend without either an electoral check by affected tax-payers or close parliamentary supervision is a recipe for irresponsible government. But, so closely will the Assembly be overseen with respect to those matters at the heart of the devolution issue, that political discontent can do little else than increase. For all the formal trappings of power, the new

Assembly will be able to do little to change the situation in Scotland. Most of the important financial and industrial decisions will still be taken outside Scotland and the Scottish Assembly will have little control over them. If the aim of creating the Assembly is to restructure Scottish society and economy by giving Scotland a legislature more responsive to regional needs, then it will surely fail. The new Assembly will not have the tools to do the job.

But this is not the aim. The aim is to stem the tide of nationalism. The Scotland Bill is a gamble. Should it succeed in placating moderate opinion in Scotland and thus reduce the level of SNP support, then the formula could succeed. If the new Assembly is dominated by Labour, Conservative, or Liberal forces, an accord with the Westminster Parliament will be possible. The parties themselves will act as institutional linkages between the two legislatures to reduce the level of conflict. It seems unlikely, however, that SNP support will wither away with such rapidity. The belief that SNP support will erode quickly once a moderate degree of devolution is granted rests on the fact that many SNP supporters are less extreme than the Party itself. While the Party aims for independence, many of its followers desire something less. But many Labour supporters have severe misgivings about Labour policy with respect to nationalization, yet remain loyal to the Party. Similarly, only a minority of Francophone supporters of the Parti Québécois want Quebec to separate from the rest of Canada, yet electoral support was sufficient for the PQ to gain control of the provincial government. Further, since gaining control, the number of Francophones wanting independence has risen. It should be recognized that the SNP is a permanent part of the political landscape. The existence of a Scottish Assembly further institutionalizes the SNP. The voice of nationalism will be a legitimate voice as never before. The SNP will exploit the situation, blaming 'London' government for the ills that will continue to beset Scotland, and demand more power to deal with Scottish problems. Eventually they may get it, but by then it may be too late to preserve the United Kingdom. It would have been far better had the Scotland Bill proposed full federalism. A Scottish Assembly responsible and answerable to a Scottish electorate would have been restrained from legislative utopianism, and a great deal of unnecessary bad feeling and conflict would have been avoided.

The Westminster Parliament has deferred decision on the question of devolution for as long as it felt it could. Finally action has been taken. But, just as the hope that a moderate degree of devolution will dish the nationalists is chimerical, so also is the persisting belief that it will eventually fade with an improvement in the British economy. After many years of economic difficulty, with the British economy in a state of permanent crisis, there are signs of recovery. The rate of inflation is falling, the balance of payments is improving, while the pound is strengthening. Unemployment remains unacceptably high, while industry still generally operates well below capacity. Eventually, it is hoped, the Scottish economy will also pick up. But this is unlikely to cause nationalism to decline. It is just as likely to increase Scottish self-confidence and belief in themselves. During the nineteenth century, and perhaps up to around 1921, the Scottish industrial economy was one of the more advanced sectors of the British economy, and yet in the years following 1880 nationalism nearly succeeded in its aim of gaining a Scottish legislature with substantial powers. Similarly in Belgium, Flemish militancy has increased with the economic development of Flanders. Throughout the nineteenth and first half of the twentieth century, Flanders was economically under-developed when compared to French-speaking Wallonia. There were numerous movements and organizations devoted to the cause of greater Flemish autonomy, but the real progress has been made since the Second World War when, with a great deal of foreign investment, the Flemish economy took off. Economic development, higher wages, industrialization, have not had the effect of dampening down regional dissidence, but have had a reverse effect. Further examples could be drawn from Nigeria, or Spain, but that would be to labour the point. The point is that the unionist can take little comfort from the prospect of economic recovery in Scotland.

Perhaps one of the better consequences of the current legislation is that it defers the possibility of violence in Scotland that has been predicted by some commentators. Nationalism, though rationally argued in economic terms, is an emotive topic. A nationalist movement, however democratic the aspirations of the leadership, carries with it on its fringes an extremist element who consider constitutionalism and the ballot box an impediment to rapid progress. The SNP has had these elements, but in the past has always dissociated itself from them, even to the extent of expelling them from the party. The danger of violence is most when the legitimate and democratic spokesman loses the political initiative in spite of popular support and becomes impotent to advance the cause. As long as the SNP can claim that the constitutional path is the most probable strategy to succeed, the wild men will be kept in check. In such circumstances they will have no moral case or support and will do the cause more harm than good. However, it is possible to envisage circumstances where violence can be considered probable. Should the current legislation fail, which is still possible, then the dashing of raised hopes and expectations could prove disastrous. The wild men may believe then that violence is the only way, and will point to the failure of constitutional attempts to achieve change as evidence.

Devolution to Scotland or Wales may also have consequences for the organization of government in England. The SNP have somewhat arrogantly claimed that this would be one of the beneficial effects of their activities. Devolution may have the effect of stimulating demands for greater autonomy from the English regions. With a Scottish Assembly as the potential government of a future independent Scotland, with the SNP threatening the parliamentary seats of the other parties, and with the gross political over-representation which will be exaggerated by the creation of a Scottish Assembly, Scotland will have a powerful lever for extracting from Westminster more than her share of government expenditure. It is unlikely that the less prosperous English regions will take kindly to such inequitable distribution of much needed resources. Recently, local-government re-organization has created large regional councils from which demands for greater autonomy may emanate. The strength of such demands will be very much weaker than in Scotland, for there is no cultural cleavage in England sufficient to throw up a regional party with any degree of political muscle. Yorkshiremen and Lancastrians may have their differences on the cricket pitch, but their sense of cultural identity is not to be compared with that of Scotsmen.

Yet, while the demands for increased English regional autonomy, and even federalism, will not carry the political weight of the Scottish demand, they should not be ignored. There are a number of related arguments that many people find quite persuasive. For example, prior to the First World War, one of the arguments that legislators at Westminster found most persuasive was that, with the increase of government business, Parliament found it more and more difficult conscientiously to scrutinize legislation. Hence the role of Parliament as a control on the executive was being eroded. Devolution was seen as one method of reducing the work-load on parliamentarians, thus giving them more time to spend on the most important matters of state. If this was true in 1913, it might also be relevant today. Further, it has been argued that devolution would considerably enhance the operation of the democratic principle in British society. Over the past half-century the duties government has taken upon itself have expanded enormously. Along with the growth of societal functions performed under the auspices of government, has come increasing governmental control of social resources. Three points can follow from this. Firstly, that it is unhealthy for the control of the material resources of society to rest in so few hands, since the control of resources creates power and the excessive control of people. The alternative is to set up countervailing centres of power with independent rights to the control of resources, hence limiting central government. This principle is found enshrined in the American Constitution. A second point deals with the amount of control of government that 'the people' are able to exercise. According to the most cynical view, this amounts merely to the right to choose by ballot between competing teams of potential governors. Sometimes this is buttressed by the suggestion that 'the people' in reality are influential minorities. It is to these that government responds rather than the public at large. By breaking up the power structure, it becomes more difficult for special interests to dominate and, because the political units are closer to the man in the street and his immediate needs, they will be that much more responsive. Thirdly, it is suggested that centralized control, and the bureaucracy it founds, is necessarily unresponsive to local needs and conditions. Legislation appropriate to London and the industrial Midlands may be very unhelpful to Humberside or Cornwall, where the problems may be very different. Extensive devolution, with increased revenue-raising powers and autonomous spheres of action, is posited as a corrective to bureaucratic uniformity. The arguments for federalism are contentious. Here only a few are given in brief and simple form. But, since the question of English regional parliaments is likely to arise, the point of view of the federalist should be fully considered if only because the issue is of such prime importance.

The problem of devolution within the United Kingdom has a long way to go before a final solution is reached. Partly this is due to consequences likely to flow from the current legislation. According to this view, devolution will become an even more central political issue. Yet, strangely, the level of debate surrounding the issue has been remarkably low, given that the implications of devolution to Scotland and elsewhere are potentially of such basic constitutional importance. The British political style is sometimes labelled 'pragmatic' in that questions of principle are eschewed in favour of immediate practicalities. Yet it is pragmatism that has got us to our present position, where legislation is approaching the statute book that few people like or want and which is dangerous to the unity of the United Kingdom. In future public debate about devolution it is to be hoped that rather more stress is laid upon fundamental questions. We should, for example, be considering the type of democracy we want, the nature of government, or whether we abandon the historically sanctified principle of the sovereignty of Parliament, perhaps in favour of a written constitution judicially interpreted, fundamental law, and a bill of rights. These are far more important and relevant questions to be considering than the immediate political difficulties facing particular political parties, for we cannot hope to solve the intricate problems devolution poses without recourse to the principles of government.

Select Bibliography

For ease of reading detailed referencing of the text has been omitted. The author would, however, like to express his gratitude to those writers whose work he has drawn upon, and hopes that they will recognize their particular contributions. A more detailed bibliography, for those who would like to read further, is by Kenneth C. Fraser, *A Bibliography of the Scottish National Movement* (1844–1973), published by Douglas S. Mack (1976).

Donald Bain *The Scottish National Party from 1966 to the 1970 General Election: A Study in Electoral Participation in British General Elections* Unpublished M.Sc. Dissertation, Univ. of Strathclyde, 1972.

Jack Brand *The Scottish Assembly: Some Decision Premises* CPS Scottish/Norwegian Conference, Helensburgh, June/July 1975.

Jack Brand *The Ideology of Scottish Nationalism* ECPR Workshop on Political Behaviour, Dissent and Protest, Louvain-la-Neuve, April 1976.

R. Brooks *Scottish Nationalism: Relative Deprivation and Social Mobility* Unpublished Ph.D. Thesis, Michigan State University, 1973.

Gordon Brown (ed.) *The Red Paper on Scotland* EUSPB, 1975.

Oliver Brown *Witdom* Maclellan, 1969.

C. M. Burns *Industrial Labour and Radical Movements in Scotland in the 1790s.* Unpublished M.Sc. Thesis, Univ. of Strathclyde, 1971.

James Cornford *Anglo-Scottish Relations since 1880* CPS Scottish/Norwegian Conference, Helensburgh, June/July 1975.

Sir R. Coupland *Welsh and Scottish Nationalism: A Study* Collins, 1954.

D. W. Crowley 'The Crofters Party, 1885–1892' *The Scottish Historical Review*, no. 119, April 1956, pp. 110–26.

Economist Intelligence Unit *The Economic Effects of Scottish Independence* 1969.

Owen Dudley Edwards *et al.* *Celtic Nationalism* Routledge & Kegan Paul, 1968.

P. Beresford Ellis & Seumas Mac a'Ghobhainn *The Scottish Insurrection 1820* Gollancz, 1970.

Milton J. Esman 'The Scottish Nationalism, North Sea Oil, and the British Response' *The Waverley Papers*, Occasional Paper No. 6, Series 1, Univ. of Edinburgh, 1975.

M. N. Franklin & A. Mughan *The Decline of Class Voting in Britain 1966–70* Unpublished Paper, Univ. of Strathclyde, June 1976.

Ian Fulton 'Scottish Oil' *Political Quarterly* Vol. 45, 1974, pp. 310–22.

W. P. Grant & R. J. C. Preece 'Welsh and Scottish Nationalism' *Parliamentary Affairs*, 1968.

William Greenberg *The Flags of the Forgotten* Clifton Books, 1969.

Eric Hall *The Scottish National Party: Kilbrandon and Devolution* Unpublished M.Sc. Dissertation, Univ. of Strathclyde, 1975.

H. J. Hanham *Scottish Nationalism* Faber & Faber, 1969.

C. Harvie *Scottish Nationalism and the Second World War* Unpublished Paper, The Open University, 1976.

C. Harvie *Scotland and Nationalism: A Study of Politics and Society in Scotland 1707–Present* Allen & Unwin, 1977.

J. C. Haworth *The National Party of Scotland and the Scottish Self-Government Movement* Unpublished D.S.S. Thesis, Syracuse Univ., 1968.

Michael Hechter *Internal Colonialism: The Celtic Fringe in British National Development 1536–1966* Routledge & Kegan Paul, 1975.

B. W. Hogwood *Spatial Differentiation of Economic and Industrial Policy in the United Kingdom* Work Group on UK Politics, Univ. of Strathclyde Conference, Bearsden, Sept. 1976.

E. Hughes 'The Scottish Reform Movement and Charles Grey 1792–4: Some fresh correspondence' *The Scottish Historical Review* no. 119, April 1956, pp. 26–41.

James G. Kellas *Modern Scotland* Pall Mall Press, 1968.

James G. Kellas *The Scottish Political System* Cambridge University Press, 1973.

James G. Kellas *The Application of Federalism to the United Kingdom with Specific Reference to North Sea Oil Production and Revenues* ECPR, Louvain-la-Neuve, April 1976.

Gavin Kennedy (ed.) *The Radical Approach: Papers on an Independent Scotland* Q Press, 1976.

Gavin Kennedy *The Defence Budget of an Independent Scotland* Fletcher Paper No. 1, Andrew Fletcher Society, 1976.

Eric Linklater *The Survival of Scotland* Heinemann, 1968.

John M. MacCormick *The Flag in the Wind* Gollancz, 1955.

Neil MacCormick *Independence and Federalism after the Referendum* Fletcher Paper No. 4, Andrew Fletcher Society, 1975.

Gavin McCrone *Scotland's Economic Progress 1951–60: A Study in Regional Accounting* Allen & Unwin, 1965.

Gavin McCrone *Scotland's Future: The Economics of Nationalism* Blackwell, 1969.

Hugh MacDiarmid *A Political Speech* Reprographia, 1972.

J. D. Mackie *A History of Scotland* Penguin, 1972.

J. P. Mackintosh 'Regional Administration: Has it worked in Scotland?' *Public Administration* vol. 42, Autumn 1964, pp. 253–75.

J. P. Mackintosh *The Devolution of Power* Chatto & Windus, 1968.

Iain McLean 'The Rise and Fall of the Scottish National Party' *Political Studies* Vol. XVIII, No. 3, 1970, pp. 357–72.

Duncan H. MacNeill *The Scottish Realm* A. & J. Donaldson, 1947.

Tom McRae *North Sea Oil and the Scottish Economy* Fletcher Paper No. 2, Andrew Fletcher Society, 1976.

Richard W. Mansbach 'The Scottish National Party: A Revised Profile' *Comparative Politics* January 1973, pp. 185–210.

Stephen Maxwell *Scotland's European Alternatives* SNP Discussion Paper, May 1975.

K. Miller (ed.) *Memoirs of a Modern Scotland* Faber & Faber, 1970.

W. L. Miller *Four-way Swing in Scotland 1955–74: Pathmakers in Scottish Politics* CPS Scottish/Norwegian Conference, Helensburgh, June/July 1975.

W. L. Miller *The Connection between SNP Voting and the Demand for Scottish Self-Government* Unpublished Paper, Univ. of Strathclyde, 1976. (Forthcoming in the *European Journal of Political Research*.)

Tom Nairn 'Scotland and Europe', *New Left Review* No. 83, Jan.–Feb. 1974, pp. 57–82.

Tom Nairn 'The Three Dreams of Scottish Nationalism' *New Left Review* No. 49, May–July 1968, pp. 3–18.

Cornelius O'Leary *Celtic Nationalism: A Study in Diversity* Congress of International Political Science Assoc., Edinburgh 1976.

F. R. Oliver 'Inter-Regional Migration and Unemployment 1951–61' *Journal of the Royal Statistical Society* Series A, Vol. 127, 1964, pp. 42–69.

H. J. Paton *The Claim of Scotland* Allen & Unwin, 1968.

John Prebble *The Darien Disaster* Secker & Warburg, 1968.

G. S. Pryde *The Treaty of Union, 1707* Nelson, 1950.

G. S. Pryde *Scotland from 1603 to the Present Day* Nelson, 1962. Reprographia, 1973.

Leone Revi *History of British Commerce* John Murray, 1870.

P. W. J. Riley *The English Ministers and Scotland, 1707–1727* Univ. of London, Athlone Press, 1964.

Richard Rose *The United Kingdom as a Multi-National State* Occasional Paper No. 6, Survey Research Centre, Univ. of Strathclyde, 1970.

Richard Rose *The Future of Scottish Politics: A Dynamic Analysis* Speculative Paper, Fraser of Allander Institute, 1975.

Richard Rose *The Constitution: Are We Studying Devolution or Breakup?* British Politics Group Conference, University of Stirling, August 1976.

John E. Schwarz 'The Scottish National Party: Non-Violent Separatism and Theories of Violence' in I. K. Feierabend *et al.* (eds.) *Anger, Violence and Politics: Theories and Research* Prentice-Hall, 1972, pp. 325–41.

Scottish Council of the Labour Party *Labour's Analysis of the Economics of Separation* Glasgow, Jan. 1976.

David Simpson 'Scottish Independence: An Economic Analysis' *Upthrust Series* No. 1, SNP Publications, 1969.

Malcolm Slesser *Scotland and Energy* Fletcher Paper No. 3, Andrew Fletcher Society, 1976.

A. A. Tait *The Economics of Devolution: A Knife Edge Problem* Speculative Paper No. 2, Fraser of Allander Institute, 1975.

H. Trevor-Roper 'Sir Walter Scott and History' *The Listener,* 19 August 1971, pp. 225–32.

Keith Webb & Eric Hall *Explanations of the Rise of Political Nationalism in Scotland* ECPR, Louvain-la-Neuve, April 1976.

Alexander Wilson *The Chartist Movement in Scotland* Univ. of Manchester Press, 1976.

Alexander Wilson 'The Scottish Chartist Press' *Scottish Labour History Society Journal*, July 1971, pp. 3–17.

J. N. Wolfe (ed.) *Government and Nationalism in Scotland* Edinburgh Univ. Press, 1969.

William Wolfe *Scotland Lives: The Quest for Independence* Reprographia, 1973.

Leslie C. Wright *Scottish Chartism* Oliver & Boyd, 1973.

Douglas Young *Scotland* Cassell, 1971.

Index